TEN MODERN
IRISH PLAYWRIGHTS

GARLAND REFERENCE LIBRARY
OF THE HUMANITIES
(VOL. 153)

TEN MODERN
IRISH PLAYWRIGHTS
A Comprehensive Annotated Bibliography

Kimball King

GARLAND PUBLISHING, INC. • NEW YORK & LONDON
1979

Library of Congress Cataloging in Publication Data

King, Kimball.
    Ten modern Irish playwrights.

    (Garland reference library of the humanities; 153)
    CONTENTS: Brendan Behan.—John Boyd.—James
Douglas. [etc.]
    Includes index.
    1. English drama—Irish authors—Bibliography.
2. English drama—20th century—Bibliography. I. Title.
Z2039.D7K56 [PR8789]   016.822′9′1408   78-68289
ISBN 0-8240-9789-0

Printed on acid-free, 250-year-life paper
Manufactured in the United States of America

CONTENTS

ACKNOWLEDGMENTS

I am particularly indebted to playwright Tom Kilroy, who received me graciously in Dublin and gave me many useful suggestions about the content and format of this book. His colleague at University College and my American compatriot, Richard Burnham, arranged interviews for me and miraculously obtained elusive addresses. When I spoke with James Douglas he was kind and encouraging; and John Boyd, in the midst of completing his two most recent plays, very kindly mailed me from Belfast a list of his major primary works. Professor and playwright Robert Hogan of the University of Delaware, who for years has made outstanding scholarly contributions to Irish literary research, provided me with a list of offerings by the Proscenium Press. And my good friend Richard Finneran's volume on Anglo-Irish literature for the Modern Language Association was an invaluable early guide. George McDaniel, my research assistant, must take a large share of credit for the contents of this volume. His bibliographical master's thesis on Brendan Behan, which he wrote under my direction, formed the heart of the first section of this book. Mrs. Joyce Bradshaw typed my first manuscript draft, and Mrs. Muriel Dyer prepared the final copy.

I am grateful to the English Department at the University of North Carolina for granting me a semester's leave to complete my research and to the University Research Council and Dr. Samuel R. Williamson, Dean of Arts and Sciences, for providing me with funds to travel to Ireland. Finally, I would like to note that my first guide in Irish studies was my wife's uncle, the late Professor William Smith Clark, who wrote *The Early Irish Stage*. He would be pleased, I think, to know that Irish theatre is still flourishing.

Kimball King
Department of English
University of North Carolina
Chapel Hill, North Carolina

INTRODUCTION

The nature and range of Irish drama has always been subjected to misunderstanding in America and other parts of the world. Professors have been known to tell students that Irish drama began with Yeats, Synge, and Lady Gregory, overlooking the fact that Ireland has had a continuous dramatic tradition for centuries. Gaelic drama, or drama written in the Irish language, merits attention both aesthetically and linguistically, but it has never dominated the Irish stage. Actors there have declaimed in a dozen or so languages. Dublin is not the only Irish city with an interest in the dramatic arts, although it is home for the legendary Abbey Theatre, a symbol of the Irish literary Renaissance in this century. Cork and Listowel are also centers of theatrical activity, and North Ireland should not be omitted. Two playwrights in this volume, John Boyd from Belfast and Brian Friel from Omagh, are impressive representatives from that region. Many playwrights born in Ireland, such as Shaw or Wilde, have been considered English dramatists, not just because they chose to live in England but also because they ultimately focused their attention on English society and its problems rather than on subjects centered in their native country. Irish-born Samuel Beckett, though once influenced by Joyce, considers himself French, writes in that language, and is identified by critics with the *nouveau roman* and the Theatre of the Absurd. On the other hand, Edna O'Brien, Thomas Murphy, and Hugh Leonard are in some sense expatriates in that they choose to spend most of their time outside of Ireland. Yet as artists they draw on Irish themes and Irish characters in all their best work.

It interests me that many Irish playwrights have an alternate occupation: John B. Keane is a pub owner, James Douglas an electrician, James McKenna a sculptor, and Thomas Kilroy a professor. Perhaps that is one reason behind their convincing portraits of everyday people. Irish writers seem to belong to a loose-knit fraternity having a spirit similar to the casual camaraderie one observes among the young English playwrights, but they seem deliberately not to have styled a specific mode or "school" in the theatre. Of course, there are shared themes. Distrust of the British, whether treated satirically in the comedies or faced squarely and bitterly in some of the tragedies, is a fundamental touchstone of Irish theatre. Attitudes toward the Roman Catholic church may be varied and ambiguous, but church-related issues are more dominant here than in any other English-speaking theatre. Since much of Ireland is still rural and very poor, there is a great emphasis on culture shock in Irish plays; coming to terms with one's provincialism is often a major character motive. And while alcoholism has increased alarmingly throughout the Western world, Irish writers are especially sensitive to its implications. All the playwrights in this volume are obsessed with the social and psychological consequences of excessive drinking. Then, too, there is a lingering puritanism in sexual matters; Edna O'Brien's work has run afoul of Irish censors on numerous occasions. On the whole, the language and behavior of Irish characters are surprisingly discreet by contemporary standards. Where else but in Ireland do heroes discuss chastity or speak of having sinned? This lack of "sophistication" is frequently a dramatic advantage, for many modern cultural phenomena are dismissed as shallow trends in Irish plays. Fundamental issues—love, greed, the power of family ties— remain to hold our attention. Thus, the best plays tend to have an archetypal power. The abstract philosophical themes of Samuel Beckett and his anti-heroes' preoccupation with eroding identity are outside the ken of mainstream Irish drama. The writers in this volume have preferred to follow Brendan Behan, a man as tortured as Beckett and possibly as brilliant, but one who, despite personal unhappiness, never ceased to affirm friendship, family, nationhood, and the possibilities of human dignity. In Ireland John B. Keane is probably the best known and certainly the most popular playwright, while Brian Friel and Hugh Leonard have wider reputations outside of Ireland, and with the success of *Da* in New York, Leonard may someday be as well known as Albee or Pinter in the modern theatre. To most people Edna O'Brien is a novelist, but her outstanding work in theatre, television, and film makes her impact on all the media undeniable. At first, I had planned to include bibliographies of Mary O'Malley and Kevin Laffan in this collection, but despite their Irish-sounding names, they both choose to describe themselves and their work as English.

Unquestionably a cross-section of any population would name Synge, O'Casey, or Yeats if asked to name famous Irish play-wrights; the great writers of the early Abbey Theatre are justly respected. Next one would have to point out the contributions of Denis Johnston, Michael Molloy, Joseph Tomelty, Michael MacLiammoir, Seamus de Burca, John O'Donovan, St. John Ervine, Padraic Colum, and other major Irish dramatists of this century. Many of these men are still living and are writing for the theatre today, or are engaged in promoting the arts to some degree. My feeling is that ample bibliographical information is already available on most of these writers. I particularly wished to describe a group of writers, comparable in range and interests to the New Wave English dramatists, who will be contributing to the world theatre during the next two or three decades. The bibliographies of Kilroy, McKenna, Douglas, and Boyd are briefer than those of the other playwrights, but they are young men nearing their prime who will undoubtedly receive more critical attention. My hope is that scholars of the modern theatre and other Anglo-Irish enthusiasts will find here the germ of further study in an intriguing field.

My principal sources for groundwork are listed below. One of the major difficulties in assembling this bibliography involved the scarcity of Irish newspapers and periodicals in America. While I had easy access to these materials in the National Library in Dublin and the Trinity College Library, I discovered that very few libraries in this country had comparable holdings. It seemed pointless to list the more esoteric items since it would be next to impossible for scholars here to obtain them. In *Twenty Modern British Playwrights*, which Garland published in 1977, I annotated interviews and critical books and articles but merely listed reviews. Here, with the exception of the scholarship on Behan, secondary criticism on the new Irish playwrights is less extensive. Therefore, I have annotated only a few reviews of Behan's plays but have described a great many reviews of the other dramatists in order to provide a more complete picture of their contributions.

Abstracts of English Studies, 1958– . Boulder, Colo.: National Council of Teachers of English.

Anglo-Irish Literature: A Review of Research. New York: Modern Language Association, 1976.

Annual Bibliography of English Language and Literature, 1920– . London: Modern Humanities Research Association.

A Bibliography of Modern Irish Drama 1899–1970. Seattle: University of Washington Press.

Cambridge Bibliography of English Literature, 5 vols. Cambridge: Cambridge University Press.

Comprehensive Index to English Language Little Magazines 1890–1970. Millwood, N.Y.: Kraus-Thompson.

Contemporary Dramatists, ed. James Vinson. London: St. James Press, 1973.

Cumulative Book Index, 1928– . New York: H. W. Wilson.

Dissertation Abstracts, 1938– . Ann Arbor, Mich.: University Microfilms.

Dissertations in English and American Literature; Theses Accepted by American, British, and German Universities, 1865–1964, by Lawrence F. McNamee. New York, London: R. R. Bowker, 1968.

Drama Criticism Index by Paul Breed and Florence Sniderman. Detroit: Gale Research Co., 1972.

Dramatic Index, 1909–1949. Boston: R. W. Faxon.

Essay and General Literature Index, 1900– . New York: H. W. Wilson.

Index to Little Magazines, 1943– . Denver: Alan Swallow.

Index to Theses Accepted for Higher Degrees in the Universities of Great Britain and Ireland, 1950– . London: ASLIB.

Index Translationum, 1955–1973. Paris: Unesco Press.

International Index to Periodicals, 1970– . New York: H. W. Wilson. From vol. 19 (April 1965-March 1966) called *Social Sciences and Humanities Index*.

Irish Publishing Record, 1967–1976. Dublin: University College.

Masters Abstracts, 1962– . Ann Arbor, Mich.: University Microfilms.

New York Theatre Critics Reviews.

New York Times Index.

The New York Times Theatre Reviews.

PMLA Bibliography.

Readers' Guide to Periodical Literature, 1900– . New York: H. W. Wilson.

Subject Index to Periodicals, 1915–1961. London: The Library Association. Continued as *British Humanities Index*, 1962– .

Theatre Dissertations, ed. Frederic M. Litto. Kent, Ohio: Kent State University Press, 1969.

The Times Index.

Year's Work in English Studies, 1919– . London: The English Association.

Brendan Behan

Born February 9, 1923; Dublin, Co. Dublin; died March 20
1964.

Although he was only forty-one years old when he
died, Brendan Behan was already an international celeb-
rity. He was known as much for his eccentric behavior
and his drinking exploits as he was for his plays. Television audiences were captivated by his flamboyant personal interviews; and as a legendary self-destructive
artist who seemed to explode with energy, he was sometimes compared to Welsh poet Dylan Thomas. Behan's reputation in the theatre depends primarily on the success of
The Hostage and The Quare Fellow. Joan Littlewood's in-
novative staging was partly responsible for their appeal
to English audiences, but each play possesses a unique
combination of warmth, compassion, and vitality. His
fascination with language, especially with odd combina-
tions of provincial dialect and modern slang, his involvement with Irish political issues, and his unexpected
treatment of Celtic stereotypes make him a thoroughly
"Irish" writer, but one capable of universal impact. His
experiences as a Borstal prisoner and his membership in
the I.R.A. provided the factual basis for many of his
dramas, stories, and essays. He failed to spearhead a
"movement" in his own country, probably because his work
was so iconoclastic; but he brought new life to the Irish
stage in the 1950s and his success indirectly served as
an inspiration to most of the playwrights included in
this volume.

PRIMARY SOURCES

I. STAGE

"An Giall" (later The Hostage). Staged Dublin, 1958.

The Hostage. Staged London, 1958. London: Methuen, 1958.

_____. London: Methuen, 1959.

_____. New York: Grove Press, 1959.

_____. New York: Grove Press, 1959.

_____. In Players, 6 (1959).

_____. London: Methuen, 1962 (revised edition).

_____. In Theatre Arts, 46 (November 1962), 28-56.

_____. In The New British Drama. Ed. Henry Popkin. New York: Grove Press, 1964.

_____. (With The Quare Fellow) New York: Grove Press, 1964.

The Quare Fellow. Staged Dublin, 1955.

_____. London: Methuen, 1956.

_____. Toronto: Ryerson, 1957.

_____. New York: Grove Press, 1957.

_____. New York: Grove Press, 1957.

_____. In Esquire, 48 (August 1957), 24-69.

_____. London: Methuen, 1960.

_____. In Seven Plays of the Modern Theatre. Ed. Harold Clurman. New York: Grove Press, 1962.

_____ and The Hostage. Two Plays. New York: Grove Press, 1964.

_____. In Post-War Drama: Extracts from Eleven Plays. Ed. John Hale. London: Faber and Faber, 1966.

Richard's Cork Leg. Staged Dublin, 1972.

_____. Ed. Alan Simpson. London: Methuen, 1973.

_____. New York: Grove Press, 1974.

II. RADIO

The Big House, June 7, 1957, B.B.C. Home Service.

_____. Evergreen Review, 5 (September-October 1961), 40-63.

2

_____. In Brendan Behan's Island, 1958.

_____. In Irish Writing, 37 (Autumn 1957), 17-34.

"A Garden Party." Broadcast 1952, Radio Éireann.

"Moving Out." Broadcast 1952, Radio Éireann.

Moving Out and A Garden Party. Two Plays. Ed. Robert
    Hogan. Dixon, Ca.: Proscenium, 1957.

"The New House." In Best Short Plays of the World
    Theatre: 1958-67. Ed. Stanley Richards. New York:
    Crown, 1968.

III. FILM

Brendan Behan's Dublin, 1968.

The Quare Fellow. Written and directed by Arthur Drei-
    fuss, 1962.

IV. RECORDINGS (with catalogue numbers)

Brendan Behan on Joyce, Folkways, 1960, 9826.

The Hostage, Columbia, 1965, Dol 329.

Irish Folk Songs and Ballads, Spoken Word, 1960, Al5.

The Quare Fellow, Spoken Word, 1963, A24.

V. FICTION

"After the Wake." Points, December 1950.

Borstal Boy. London: Hutchinson, 1958.

_____. New York: A. Knopf, 1959.

_____. London: Berkeley, 1975.

_____. As adapted for the stage by Frank MacMahon.
    New York: Random House, 1971.

"Bridewell Revisited." Points, Winter 1952.

"Bridewell Revisited." (Different from the above.) <u>New</u>
<u>Statesman</u>, 8 December 1956, p. 740.

"Christmas Day in Walton Jail." <u>Irish</u> <u>Writing</u>, 35
(1956), 80-88.

"Confirmation Suit." <u>Standard</u>, Easter number, 1953.

_____. <u>Spectator</u>, 27 April 1962, pp. 547-48.

_____. <u>Atlantic</u>, 210 (August 1962), 39-42.

"Dog Race." <u>Atlantic</u>, 210 (October 1962), 57-60.

"Dogmen and Bogmen." <u>Twentieth</u> <u>Century</u>, 969 (November
1957), 419-28.

"Extract from <u>Borstal</u> <u>Boy</u>." <u>Overland</u>, 2 (Winter 1959),
41-43.

"I Become a Borstal Boy." <u>Bell</u>, 4 (June 1962), 165-70.

<u>The</u> <u>Scarperer</u>. Serialized in the <u>Irish</u> <u>Times</u>, October-
November 1953.

_____. Garden City, N.Y.: Doubleday, 1964.

_____. London: Hutchinson, 1966.

_____. London: Queen's House, 1976.

"Where We All Came into Town." <u>Evergreen</u> <u>Review</u>, 18
(May-June 1961), 18-32.

"A Woman of No Standing." <u>Envoy</u>, 3 (1950), 37-42.

"Woman on the Corner of the Next Block to Us." <u>Vogue</u>,
128 (December 1956), 85.

VI. NONFICTION

"Brendan Behan's Dublin." <u>Atlantic</u>, 210 (September 1962),
41-45.

<u>Brendan</u> <u>Behan's</u> <u>Island</u>: <u>An</u> <u>Irish</u> <u>Sketchbook</u>. London:
Hutchinson, 1958.

_____. New York: Bernard Geis, 1962.

<u>Brendan</u> <u>Behan's</u> <u>New</u> <u>York</u>. New York: Bernard Geis, 1964.

_____. London: Hutchinson, 1964.

Confessions of an Irish Rebel. London: Hutchinson, 1965.

_____. New York: Bernard Geis, 1966.

"Dublin Is Grand in the Sun." Irish Press, 26 April 1955, p. 8.

"Easter Lily." New Statesman and Nation, 9 March 1957, p. 310. [Letter]

"The English Out of Ireland." New Statesman and Nation, 8 December 1956, p. 747. [Letter]

"Foreword" to The Howards, a play by Seamus de Burca. Dublin, 1960.

"Foreword" to The Soldier's Song, by Seamus de Burca. Dublin, 1957.

"Hardy Hot and Cold." Colby Library Quarterly, 5, 66-69.

Hold Your Hour and Have Another. London: Hutchinson, 1963.

_____. Boston: Little, Brown, 1964.

Irish Press. [96 columns, March 1954-April 1955.]

"The Laughing Boy." New Statesman, 20 September 1958, pp. 384-85.

"On Broadway." Show, 1 (October 1961), 111.

"Pleascain i Sasana" ("Bombs in England"). Six articles in Comhar, October 1952-April 1953.

"Sunbathers Cover Their Faces in Sweden." Vogue, 132 (November 1958), 24-26.

"We Don't Have Leprechauns, Paddys and Magic Mists." Newsweek, 27 March 1961, p. 28.

VII. POETRY

In the 1940s and early 1950s, Behan published twelve poems written in Gaelic. Most appeared in the Irish-language magazine Comhar (the April 1964 number of Comhar reprinted nine of these; "Filleadh Mhic Eachaidh" was excluded). Selected poems in English translation may be

found in Kearney's The Writings of Brendan Behan and
O'Connor's Brendan Behan.

"Aithrige" ("Repentance"). Comhar, October 1947.

"Buichas le Joyce" ("Thanks to Joyce"). Comhar, August
    1949.

"Do Bhev" ("For Bev"). Comhar, May 1956.

"Do Shean O Suilleabhain" ("For Sean O'Sullivan").
    Comhar, August 1949.

"Filleadh Mhic Eachaidh" ("The Return of McCaughey").
    Comhar, December 1944.

"Gui An Rannaire" ("The Rimer's Prayer"). Comhar, April
    1950.

"Jackeen ag. Caoineadh na mBlascaod" ("A Jackeen Cries
    at the Loss of the Blaskets"). Comhar, August 1949.

"Jim Larkin." Comhar, March 1947.

"L'Existentialisme." Comhar, March 1952.

"Sraid Grafton" ("Grafton Street"). Feasta, August 1949.

"Teacht an Earraigh" ("The Coming of Spring"). Comhar,
    October 1951.

"Uaigneas" ("Loneliness"). Envoy, January 1950.

VIII.   TRANSLATIONS

BORSTAL BOY

    Borstal Boy. Tr. by Slobodan Petkovic. Novi Sad:
        Bratstvo-jedinstvo, 1964. Serbo-Croatian.

    Borstal Boy. Tr. by Curt Meyer-Clason. Cologne:
        Kiepenheuer and Witsch, 1963. German.

    Borstal-Gutt. Tr. by Ragnor Kuam. Oslo: Gyldendal,
        1960. Norwegian.

    Borstalpojken. Tr. by Thomas Warburton. Stockholm:
        Wahlström and Widstrand (Ny uta.), 1964. Swedish.

    En Irsk Oprører. Tr. by Mogens Boisen. Copenhagen:
        Nyt Nordisk Forlag, 1960 and 1971. Danish.

Gistend Bloed. De levensgang van Brendan Behan.
Tr. by Hans de Vries. 's-Grav: Zud-Holl, 1962. Dutch.

Poikia Vankilassa. Tr. by V. Mattila. Helsinki:
Kirjayhtymä, 1960. Finnish.

BRENDAN BEHAN'S ISLAND

Maj Zeleny Ostrov. Tr. by Elena Chmelova. Bratis-
lava: Epocha, 1969. Czechoslovakian.

CONFESSIONS OF AN IRISH REBEL

Airurando No Hangyakusha. Tr. by Osaka Osamu.
Tokyo: Shobunsha, 1972. Japanese.

Bekentenissen Van Een Ierse Rebel. Tr. by Ko Kooman.
Amsterdam: Arbeiderspers, 1970. Dutch.

Ein Gutshaus in Irland. Tr. by Annemarie and
Heinrich Böll. Berlin: Luchterhand, 1962. German.

HOLD YOUR HOUR AND HAVE ANOTHER

Bi Lidt Og Få En Til. Tr. by Georgjedde. Copenhagen: Nyt Nordisk Forlag, 1964. Danish.

Encore un verre avant de partir. Tr. by Paul-Henri
Claudel. Paris: Gallimard, 1970. French.

THE HOSTAGE

Die Geisel in Stücke Fürs Theater. Tr. by Annemarie
and Heinrich Böll. Berlin: Luchterhand, 1962. German.

Deux Otages. Tr. by Elisabeth Janvier. Paris:
Gallimard, 1961. French.

El rehen. Tr. by Ana Antón-Pacheco and Juan José
Arteche. Madrid: Edicusa, 1972. Spanish.

Gidslet. (Tragi-Operette: The Akter) Tr. by Paul
Sorensen. Copenhagen: Gyldendal, 1961. Danish.

Gizli Ordu. Tr. by Güner Sümer. Istanbul: Islen
Yayineui, 1963. Turkish.

L'ostaggio in L'impiccato de domani and L'ostaggio.
Tr. by Gigi Lunari. Milano: Feltrinelli, 1960.
Italian.

Rukojmí. Tr. by Jirí Mucha. Prague: Dilia, 1964.
Czechoslovakian.

Un Otage. Tr. by Jacqueline Sandstrum. Paris:
Avant-Scène, 1962. French.

Talec. Tr. by Ciril Kosmac. Ljubljana: "Scena,"
1972. Slovenian.

THE QUARE FELLOW

Der Mann Morgen früh in Stücke Fürs Theater. Tr. by
Annemarie and Heinrich Böll. Berlin: Luchterhand, 1962. German.

Le Client du Matin. Tr. by Jacqueline Sandstrum and
Boris Vian. Paris: Gallimard, 1959. French.

L'impiccato in L'impiccato de domani and L'ostaggio.
Tr. by Gigi Lunari. Milano: Feltrinelli, 1960. Italian.

Reggeli Üvöltés. A Tüsz. Tr. by Ilona Róna.
Budapest: Európa Kiadó, 1964. Hungarian.

Saerlingen. Radioversion ved Philip Rooney. Tr. by
Ole Sarvig. Fredensborg: Arena, 1962. Danish.

Vispera de Ejecucion. Tr. by Ana Antón-Pacheco and
Juan José Arteche. Madrid: Edicusa, 1972. Spanish.

THE SCARPERER

Der Spanner. Tr. by Annemarie and Heinrich Böll.
Frankfurt: Buchergilde Gutenberg, 1969. German.

El Escurridizo. Tr. by Maria R. Sanagustín.
Barcelona: Caralt, 1968. Spanish.

L'Escarpeur. Tr. by Paul-Henri Claudel. Paris:
Gallimard, 1968. French.

Ucieczka. Tr. by Waclaw Niepokólczycki. Warsaw:
Czytelnik, 1970. Polish.

IX. INTERVIEWS

Atkinson, Brooks. "Behan Boxes the Conversational Com-
pass from People to Plays to Bar Mitzvahs." New
York Times, 9 December 1960, p. 28.
    Behan holds forth in a New York bar. He dis-
cusses, among other things, the police, J. P.

Donleavy, the Catholic Church, <u>Richard's Cork Leg</u>,
World War II, John Kennedy, and his own alcoholism.

Calta, Louis. "Behan Comments on the Theatre." <u>New York
Times</u>, 3 September 1960, p. 8.
    Behan talks about politics, sin, "a writer's
duty," his origins, his work in jail ("Anything
written in jail is rubbish, and that includes <u>Pil-
grim's Progress</u>"), and his drinking.

Gelb, Arthur. "Brendan Behan's Sober Side." <u>New York
Times</u>, 18 September 1960, II:1.
    Behan discusses "the catacombs," his long-
planned, never-finished novel: "It's about a lot of
no-gooders or harmless people." He also touches on
beatniks·and O'Casey and O'Neill.

Weatherby, W. J. "But Not in the Pejorative Sense."
<u>Guardian</u>, 4 March 1960, p. 9.
    Weatherby "interviews" Behan during another
tour of Dublin's pubs. Behan repeats one of his
favorite assertions that "the author's duty is to
let down his country." Despite Weatherby's attempts
to get him to "talk literature," Behan continually
reverts to pub-talk with the patrons. Weatherby
concludes the aborted interview with the observation
that Behan is "essentially a warm-hearted, sensitive
man putting his armor on again."

X. INTERVIEWS--TV

May 1956, <u>Panorama</u> (B.B.C.), with Malcolm Muggeridge.
    This is one of the most famous interviews in
television history. Having arrived too drunk to
speak coherently, Behan sang instead. He had gotten
through "The Old Triangle" (from <u>The Quare Fellow</u>)
and begun "The Red Flag," when he was hustled off
the stage. Muggeridge, far from being upset, later
called the occasion "the pleasantest and most rewarding evening I ever spent in Lime Grove." And
Behan, in the words of his biographer O'Connor,
"became a folk hero overnight."

9 November 1959, <u>Small World</u> (CBS), with Ed Murrow.
    This was Behan's first interview on American
TV. He, literary critic John Mason Brown, and comic
actor Jackie Gleason were scheduled to speak on "The
Art of Conversation" via a three-way telephone hook-
up. Behan, again too drunk to speak coherently, was
eliminated halfway through. Gleason later remarked:
"Behan was coming through a hundred per cent proof."

10 October 1960, The Jack Paar Show, with guest host
   Arlene Francis.
      This was a very successful interview for Behan.
   He discussed New York critics, American politics,
   and his favorite, "an author's duty to let down his
   country." In addition to Behan, the show featured
   Constance Cummings, Arthur Schlesinger, Jr., and
   Jimmy Kirkwood, Jr.

17 October 1960, Open End, with David Susskind.
      Behan appeared with Tony Richardson, Tennessee
   Williams, Jack Lemmon, Celeste Holm, and Anthony
   Quinn. He discussed the police, sex on the stage,
   and religion, getting a riotous "avalanche of laugh-
   ter" from this last by reciting a ribald verse about
   a Protestant minister.

31 October 1960, The Jack Paar Show, with Jack Paar.
      Behan discussed The Hostage and the popular
   reaction to it. According to O'Connor: "He agreed
   with Aldous Huxley that people who are shocked [by
   the play] are the very people who wanted to be
   shocked."

SECONDARY SOURCES

I. CRITICISM

Alvarez, A. "The Anti-Establishment Drama." Partisan
   Review, 26 (Fall 1959), 606-11.
      Alvarez includes Behan with John Osborne, Ar-
   nold Wesker, and Shelagh Delaney as one of the "four
   most promising playwrights" of the anti-establishment school. He thinks that The Hostage is superior
   to Dylan Thomas' Under Milk Wood because of its
   "straightforwardness of pity and gusto."

Armstrong, William A. Experimental Drama. London: G.
   Bell, 1963. Pp. 79-102.
      Armstrong looks at plays by O'Casey, Behan, and
   Thomas Murphy. He finds that The Quare Fellow re-
   sembles the plays of O'Casey's first phase in its
   "enveloping [of] a perennial myth in a naturalistic
   setting." The Hostage, on the other hand, is deliberately anti-naturalistic in style, though its
   theme is much like that of The Quare Fellow.

_____. "A Wreath for Brendan Behan." _Irish Digest_,
May 1964, pp. 81-84.
    This is a collection of obituaries in primarily
Irish newspapers written by one-time colleagues or
admirers of Behan. However, comments by Joan Littlewood of the _Observer_ and W. R. Rogers of the _Sun-
day Times_ are also included.

"Banking Success." _Time_, 8 December 1958, p. 50.
    This is a portrait of Behan, replete with one-
liners.

"Beating the Gargle." _Theatre Arts_, 47 (February 1963),
9.
    This describes Behan's efforts to combat his
alcoholism.

Behan, Beatrice. _My Life with Brendan_. Los Angeles:
Nash, 1974.
    This is a lucid, moving memoir by Behan's
widow, profusely illustrated with photographs. It
is perhaps the best available picture of Behan's
last years.

Behan, Brian. "Brendan." _Spectator_, 17 July 1964, 77-79.
    Excerpted from _With Breast Expanded_, this is a
beautifully written personal memoir. Brian attempts
to explain why his brother willfully sought an early
death. His answer: Brendan had become disenchanted
with the Republican Movement and with the people who
claimed to be his friends. He was renowned, but the
acclaim seemed to be mere empty flattery: "To make
a god of someone is to destroy them as surely as
driving a knife into their back."

_____. _With Breast Expanded_. London: MacGibbon and
Kee, 1964.
    This is an autobiography of Brendan's brother.
It discusses all the Behans, including Brendan.

Behan, Dominic. _My Brother Brendan_. London: Frewin,
1965.
    Though this contains some entertaining anec-
dotes, it reveals more about Dominic than Brendan.
The two were often unfriendly rivals, and Dominic's
bitterness frequently shows through.

_____. "Posterity and After." _Spectator_, 29 April
1960, pp. 619-20.
    Dominic strikes out again at brother Brendan.
In this short vignette describing the opening night
of Dominic's play, _Poverty Be Damned_, he recounts
how a certain "big man" doffed his hat, rose un-
steadily to his feet, and crashed down in a drunken

stupor. At the play's end, the big man awoke and
pronounced: "Rubbish."

_____. Teems of Times and Happy Returns. London:
Frewin, 1961. (Reprinted in the U.S. as Tell Dublin
I Miss Her, 1962.)
        This is a history of the Behan family in novel
form.

Bergner, Heinz. "Brendan Behan: The Hostage (1958)." In
    Das zeitgenossische englische Drama: Einfuhrung,
    Interpretation, Dokumentation. Eds. Klaus-Dieter
    Fehse and Norbert Platz. Frankfurt: Athenäum,
    1965. Pp. 86-100.

Borel, Françoise. "Alas, Poor Brendan!" In Aspects of
    the Irish Theatre. Eds. Patrick Rafroidi, et al.
    Paris: Editions Universitaires, Pubs. de l'Univ. de
    Lille, 1972. Pp. 119-36.
        This is a rather slight attempt at serious
    criticism. Borel looks at The Quare Fellow and The
    Hostage and gives plot summaries of each, inter-
    spersing them with short quotations from reviews.
    She notes the similarity of The Hostage to Frank
    O'Connor's "Guests of the Nation," and places the
    tone and style of both plays in the music hall tra-
    dition.

Boyle, Ted E. Brendan Behan. New York: Twayne, 1969.
        Boyle provides a good biographical sketch of
    Behan in the first half of this book. He also gives
    plot summaries and interpretations of all his works.

Browne, Joseph. See Friel below.

Brustein, R. S. Seasons of Discontent. New York: Simon
    and Schuster, 1965. Pp. 177-80.
        Brustein links Behan with Ionesco and Brecht
    rather than with the traditionalist O'Casey. He
    thinks Behan has breathed new life into the theatre.

Buchoh, Paul G. "Brendan Behans The Hostage: Lachende
    Hinnahme einer bittern und chaotischen Welt."
    Literatur in Wissenschaft und Unterricht, 4 (1971),
    215-36.
        Translated into English the title reads: "The
    Laughing Acceptance of a Bitter and Chaotic World."
    Buchoh claims that, though the play appears chaotic,
    it actually presents Behan's vision of the world
    seen with love and laughter despite its chaos and
    senseless values. (In German.)

12

Burgess, Anthony. "The Writer as Drunk." Spectator,
    4 November 1966, p. 588.
        Burgess compares Behan to Dylan Thomas. Both
    pub-men, they were rhetorical writers with "an an-
    cestral memory for the word-man's social function,
    the bardic job." For them, pub-drinking remained
    the last of our creative social acts.

Cahill, Susan and Thomas. A Literary Guide to Ireland.
    New York: Scribner's, 1973. Pp. 6, 274, 305-12.
        The Cahills consider Behan a great Irish writer
    and devote a section to his life in Dublin, pointing
    out his favorite pubs and noting some well-known
    anecdotes about the playwright.

Callery, S. "Brendan Behan: The Ignominy of Success."
    Commonweal, 93 (1970), 87-91.
        This is a fond remembrance of Behan. Callery
    addresses the question of why Behan drank himself to
    death. He theorizes that Behan felt himself increas-
    ingly estranged from the people he loved best, the
    lower classes. Out of loneliness, he drank more and
    more: "He was a man on the way to the loving arms
    of Jesus and he wooed death passionately."

Caulfield, Max. "A Portrait of Brendan Behan Drinking
    Life's Last Bitter Dregs." Fact, 3 (1966), 18-25.
        The author accompanied Behan on a disagreeable
    drinking tour of Dublin shortly before Behan's death.
    The alcoholic ruin of the artist is portrayed.

Chiari, J. Landmarks of Contemporary Drama. London:
    Herbert Jenkins, 1965. Pp. 110, 133.
        Chiari briefly notes Joan Littlewood's collabo-
    ration with Behan and includes the latter in a list
    of playwrights who follow John Osborne in portraying
    "rootless individuals unhappy and at war with the
    social order."

Childers, Roderick W. "Brendan Behan." Chicago Today,
    3 (Winter 1966), 50-54.
        Childers, another of Behan's seemingly endless
    supply of posthumous friends, retells a few of his
    favorite Brendan-stories.

Clurman, Harold. The Naked Image. New York: Macmillan,
    1966. Pp. 43-44.
        Clurman writes of The Hostage that it is "an
    improvisation in beat time." He comments on the
    special collaborative nature of the play and consid-
    ers it a "product of that state of mind which makes
    for beatniks the world over."

Cole, Joseph. "Brendan." Books and Bookmen, 13 (November 1967), 34-35.
      This is a reminiscence, less convincing than most. Cole claims that Behan often did not fill the central role of the incidents he was involved in. The few stories he relates do not bear this out.

_____. "Brendan I Hardly Knew You." Quadrant, 59 (1969), 46-50.
      This is another printing of "Brendan" above.

_____. "Night Out in Dublin." London Magazine, 5 (November 1965), 23-35.
      This is a description of a night of drinking with Behan. It reveals the strained relationship of Brendan and his brother Dominic.

_____. "Night Out in Dublin." Meanjin, 27 (September 1968), 309-14.
      This is the same as above.

Coogan, Tim Pat. "Closing Time." Spectator, 27 March 1964, p. 406.
      This is a brief lament at Behan's passing describing the feeling in Dublin after his death: there is "a general consciousness of a gap that won't be filled easily, if at all."

Cronin, Sean. "Baggot Street Bard." Commonweal, 12 January 1968, pp. 447-48.
      This is a portrait of Patrick Kavanagh, "perhaps Ireland's greatest contemporary poet." He had "made a steadfast stand against what he called 'Behanism.'"

_____. "Sting-a-ling-a-ling." Nation, 13 May 1968, pp. 642-44.
      Cronin reviews Rae Jeffs' book, Brendan Behan. He catalogs what he feels was Behan's best work: Borstal Boy, The Quare Fellow, The Hostage, the short story "Confirmation Suit," and the unfinished Richard's Cork Leg. Jeffs, he says, staged with Behan an unsuccessful attempt to "save" him. He feels that Behan, like the dead English soldier Leslie in The Hostage, triumphed over death in the end.

_____. "Where the Martyrs Died." Nation, 7 November 1966, pp. 486-88.

Davies, M. Bryn. "A Few Thoughts about Milk Wood." Literary Half-Yearly, 5 (January 1964), 41-44.
      Davies writes of Dylan Thomas' Under Milk Wood. The play's obsession with death places it outside the tradition of Behan, Synge, and O'Casey.

Davies, Stan. "Shed a Tear for Brendan." Saturday
Night, 79 (May 1964), 16-18.
This is a fond, though somewhat bitter obituary.
The author recounts a few Behan anecdotes he has
heard from various friends of Brendan.

de Burca, Seamus. Brendan Behan: A Memoir. Newark, Delaware: Proscenium Press, 1971.
This is a personal memoir by Behan's cousin.
de Burca gives us a first-hand look at some of
Brendan's escapades and at the Behan family in general. Particularly interesting is his history of
Behan's early efforts at writing and publishing.

_____. "The Essential Brendan Behan." Modern Drama,
8 (1966), 374-81.
This is an excerpt from the above.

Delehantz, James. "Six Hours with Brendan." Kilkenny
Magazine, 2 (Autumn 1960), 41-44.
This is a personal anecdote revealing the sober
reflective nature underneath Behan's riotous mask.

Duprey, Richard A. "The Bloodshot World of Brendan
Behan." Critic, 20 (December 1961-January 1962),
55-57.
Duprey says that Behan's world-view reveals an
immense sympathy with suffering humanity; his free
language emphasizes his stand as a believer in the
freedom of the human spirit.

"End to Confusion." Newsweek, 30 March 1964, p. 72.
This is an obituary for Behan, including a re-
capitulation of his life and some significant
quotes.

Eriksson, Lars-Goran. "Brendan Behans universitet."
Horisont, 18, 56-64, n.d.

Fallis, Richard. The Irish Renaissance. Syracuse:
Syracuse University Press, 1977. Pp. 141, 172, 181,
259, 265, 268-70.
Fallis frequently praises Behan's "brilliant
instincts for theatre." He analyzes The Quare Fellow and The Hostage, notes the lyrical but "authentic" talk of Behan's characters. The author's autobiography and early censorship problems are also
cited.

Farragher, Bernard. "Brendan Behan's Unarranged Realism."
Drama Critique, 4 (February 1961), 38-39.
Farragher maintains that The Hostage reveals
Behan's debt to O'Casey. O'Casey also creates out
of apparent chaos plays which are simultaneously

pictures and interpretations of life.

Fitzgerald, Maurice. "Half an Evening with Brendan."
    Canadian Forum, 39 (October 1959), 147-48.
        This is an account of a riotous evening spent
    drinking with Behan in a Dublin pub.

Friedrich, Otto. "Chronicle of a Small Beer." Reporter,
    19 March 1959, pp. 45-46.
        Friedrich reviews Borstal Boy but begins with a
    personal reminiscence of Brendan: "In his hunger
    for approval, in his wild storytelling imagination,
    his jubilation over tiny victories and his rage over
    tiny defeats, he was like an overgrown child. . . ."

"Gay Irish Insults." Life, 19 September 1960, p. 51.
        This is an editorial describing one of Behan's
    attacks on New York City.

Gerdes, Peter R. The Major Works of Brendan Behan.
    Bern: Herbert Lang, 1973.
        This is one of the most important surveys of
    Behan's work as a whole. Written initially as a
    doctoral dissertation, it is a highly organized and
    carefully detailed analysis of The Quare Fellow,
    Borstal Boy, An Giall, and The Hostage. Gerdes
    analyzes character, plot, theme, and style of each.
    He also provides a good history of the writing, and,
    in the case of the plays, the production of each of
    the works. Particularly interesting is his compari-
    son of An Giall to its English translation, The
    Hostage.

Hackett, Walter. "Brendan Behan." Critic, 22 (1964),
    48-51.
        This is another account of another drinking
    tour of Dublin with Behan, containing the usual
    quips and gargles.

Harmon, Maurice. "The Era of Inhibitions: Irish Litera-
    ture 1920-60." Emory University Quarterly, 22
    (Spring 1966), 18-28.
        The author describes the conditions in Ireland
    after the Revolution, which were particularly bad
    for the writer. Much of the Irish literature since
    has dealt with the effects of the inhibitions on the
    individual and the nation. Behan, however, repre-
    sents a new group of writers who have shown evidence
    of clearing the air of "stodgy nationalism and stale
    piety."

Hatch, Robert. "The Roaring Presence of Brendan Behan."
    Horizon, 3 (January 1961), 113-14.
        Hatch writes that Behan should not be grouped--

as he often is--with contemporary rebellious writers
like Beckett, Genet, and Osborne, because his work
has a distinctly different bent. While the others'
rebelliousness is lonely and individualistic,
Behan's is social and "revolutionary." The Hostage
reveals his basic optimism and love.

Hays, H. R. "Transcending Naturalism." Modern Drama,
    5 (May 1962), 27-36.
    Hays examines the ways new British dramatists
    "transcend naturalism." Behan does it by the use of
    poetic devices that reveal his attacks on the Estab-
    lishment and his sympathy for "ordinary humanity."

Hewes, Henry. See McKenna below.

Hogan, Robert. After the Irish Renaissance. Minneapolis:
    University of Minnesota Press, 1967. Pp. 198-207.
    Hogan concentrates on the themes of The Quare
    Fellow (which he compares to Shaw's Major Barbara)
    and The Hostage (compared to Gay's The Beggar's
    Opera). He also touches on the lesser works and in-
    cludes some rare praise for The Scarperer.

_____. "Dublin: The Summer Season and the Theatre
    Festival, 1967." See Friel below.

_____, Bonnie K. Scott and Gordon Henderson. "The Mod-
    ern Drama." In Anglo-Irish Literature: A Review of
    Research. Ed. Richard J. Finneran. New York:
    Modern Language Association, 1976. Pp. 528, 530-31,
    548, 550-51, 558-60.
    This article outlines Behan's career and his
    impact on Irish drama in general. He is credited
    with revitalizing the drama of his day. Individual
    plays by Behan as well as his general themes and
    techniques are discussed.

Hunt, Albert. "A Game No More." New Society, 8 June
    1972, p. 524.
    Hunt views the revival of The Hostage in the
    light of the current (1972) political situation.
    He finds that, with the rise of violence connected
    with the I.R.A., Behan's play has taken on a "spuri-
    ous contemporaneity" and the events it portrays are
    no longer joking matters.

Hynes, Sam. "An Irish Success." Commonweal, 4 March
    1960, pp. 627-29.
    Hynes claims that Behan's plays and autobiog-
    raphy deal with only two subjects: "prison life and
    the I.R.A." His plays have no plots; their greatest
    virtue lies in the dialogue. Thus far his work is
    only promising.

17

"Irishman on a Rampage." Newsweek, 23 February 1959,
    pp. 105-06.
        A Newsweek staffer accompanied Behan on a
    drinking tour of Dublin, the most fruitful result of
    which being the playwright's quip: "I write to keep
    myself in liquor."

Jeffs, Rae. Brendan Behan: Man and Showman. London:
    Hutchinson, 1966.
        The first of the Behan biographies, this covers
    only that time from the height of his success in the
    late Fifties until his death. Mrs. Jeffs was
    Behan's editor at Hutchinson's and was largely re-
    sponsible for the bulk of his output in the later
    part of his life. This book describes that period
    sympathetically and honestly, and makes us aware of
    the tragic waste of Behan's life.

Kazin, Alfred. "The Causes Go, the Rebels Remain." At-
    lantic Monthly, 203 (June 1959), 65-67.
        Kazin states that Behan's working-class back-
    ground has freed him from literary convention. He
    uses the language of the streets. As Borstal Boy
    reveals, he is intensely aware of life around him
    and is at the same time one of its most vital re-
    flectors.

Kearney, Colbert. The Writings of Brendan Behan. Dublin:
    Gill and Macmillan, 1977.
        This is probably the most important single ex-
    ample of Behan criticism yet to appear. Kearney
    provides clear and detailed analyses of The Quare
    Fellow, Borstal Boy, and The Hostage. There is also
    a chapter on Behan's Gaelic poetry. As a work of
    sustained criticism, this is superior to the earlier
    offerings by Boyle and Gerdes for it avoids the pit-
    falls of academic formalism into which those works
    sometimes fall.

Kenney, Herbert A. Literary Dublin: A History. Dublin:
    Gill and Macmillan, 1974. Pp. 18, 151, 225, 239-40,
    283-89, 301, 316.
        An understanding of Behan and Beckett, such
    vastly different authors, provides a key to the
    paradoxes of modern Irish life. Behan is called the
    literary heir of Oliver St. John Gogarty. A brief
    biography is provided and most of his works are men-
    tioned, though not analyzed in detail.

Kerr, Walter. The Theatre in Spite of Itself. New York:
    Simon and Schuster, 1963. Pp. 120-23.
        Kerr discusses The Hostage, commenting on the
    music hall nature of the production.

Kiely, Benedict. "That Old Triangle: A Memory of Brendan
    Behan." Hollins Critic, 2 (February 1965), 1-12.
    This is a portrait of Behan: gregarious,
    chronically restless, with a kindly and wildly comic
    spirit. It traces his career with the I.R.A. and
    his subsequent imprisonment.

Kilroy, Thomas. "Groundwork for an Irish Theatre,"
    Studies: An Irish Quarterly Review (Dublin), 48
    (Summer 1959), 192-98.
    "Whatever his talents . . . Brendan Behan could
    not . . . be considered representative of a whole
    new movement in Irish writing--[he] stands almost
    alone in the Irish theatre today, that is, if he has
    anything to do with it."

Kitchin, Laurence. Drama in the Sixties: Form and Inter-
    pretation. London: Faber and Faber, 1966. Pp. 98,
    106.
    Kitchin, in noting Irish-born A. E. F. Horni-
    man's role in extending the Abbey Theatre's influ-
    ence to Manchester, England, claims that the first
    commercial success of Littlewood's Theatre Workshop
    was Behan's The Hostage. Behan's plays are in the
    O'Casey tradition according to Kitchin.

_____. Mid-Century Drama. London: Faber and Faber,
    1966. Pp. 23, 24, 110, 111.
    Kitchin praises Behan as a leader of the "new
    drama." The Hostage, though frivolous in tone and
    facilely constructed, communicates wisdom and pathos.
    Kitchin feels Joan Littlewood's staging of The Hos-
    tage at the theatre workshop is the most "informedly
    Brechtian work yet done in English."

Kleinstuck, Johannes. "Brendan Behan's The Hostage."
    Essays and Studies, 24 (1971), 60-82.
    Kleinstuck maintains that The Hostage must be
    understood in reference to Irish history and poli-
    tics. Behan should not be compared to Brecht, as he
    sometimes is, because he does not attempt to change
    the world through the theatre.

Koziol, Herbert. "Zur literarischen Verwendung des
    Rhyming Slang." Archiv für Das Studium Die Neueren
    Sprachen und Literatur, 117 (August 1965), 105-08.
    Koziol makes the point that authors who use
    rhyming slang are usually aware of the difficulty of
    making themselves understood. Borstal Boy provides
    examples of the hints which a reader may look for to
    aid in the deciphering of slang.

Krause, David. "The Barbarous Sympathies of Antic Irish
Comedy." Malahat Review, 22 (April 1972), 99-117.
    Krause finds in Irish drama the recurrent theme
of comic profanation: i.e., the anarchic liberating
release which comes from grotesque and irrational
behavior. The Hostage provides a clear example.

Levidova. I. "A New Hero Appears in the Theatre (Notes
on Young Dramatists in England)." Inostrannaya
Literatura, 1 (January 1962), 201-08.
    Behan is seen as one of a number of the new
"plebeian heroes," introduced by Osborne in Look
Back in Anger. These new playwrights attempt to ex-
press objectively their reflection of life, whose
ugly aspects arouse in them feelings of protest.

Levitt, Paul M. "Hostages to History: Title as Dramatic
Metaphor in The Hostage." Die Neueren Sprachen,
n.s. 24, (1975), 401-06.
    Levitt claims that The Hostage is an attack on
the Irish devotion to the past and the failed dream
of unifying northern and southern Ireland. The
title is a dramatic metaphor for the mad devotion
to an empty dream which makes hostages out of the
characters in the play.

Linehan, Fergus. "Four Irish Playwrights." Irish Digest,
74 (April 1962), 84-87.
    Linehan says that, though Behan is the most
popular Irish playwright abroad, in Ireland that
distinction belongs to the melodramatic John B.
Keane. Donagh MacDonagh and James McKenna are
also discussed.

MacAnna, Tomas. "The Villon of Dublin." Times Literary
Supplement, 15 July 1977, p. 850.
    This is a review of Kearney's The Writings of
Brendan Behan. MacAnna praises the work's complete-
ness and readability but doubts that anyone will
ever be able to explain Behan's "exuberant self-
destructing talent."

MacAonghusa, Proinsias. "Passing of Stephen B." New
Statesman, 21 July 1967, pp. 82-83.
    This is an account of the wake for Brendan's
father. An I.R.A. comrade of Brendan's is quoted:
"Jaysus, if there is another world, the language
there must be shocking tonight with Stephen and
Brendan having a party!"

MacDonagh, Donagh. "Behans Abroad, Being the Subject
Matter of a Talk from Radio Eireann." Kilkenny
Magazine, 12-13 (Spring 1965), 55-60.
    MacDonagh accompanied Behan on a trip abroad.
This is an account of their journey.

MacInnes, Colin. "The Writings of Brendan Behan." <u>London</u>
<u>Magazine</u>, 2 (August 1962), 53-61.
　　MacInnes claims that Behan is "the only writer
of his time who will be read a century from now."
<u>Borstal Boy</u> and <u>The Quare Fellow</u> reveal him as a
tragic artist, infused with deep warmth for the
plight of all men. He is a revolutionary humanist
concerned with the oppressed everywhere.

MacIntyre, Thomas. "This Dying Lark." <u>Kenyon Review</u>, 27
(Winter 1965), 152-55.
　　MacIntyre reviews Behan's major works. <u>Borstal</u>
<u>Boy</u>, as an autobiographical novel, was ideally suit-
ed to Behan. It allowed him to "go on a rampage,"
presenting "the insuperable zest of Dublin lane and
highway. . . ." <u>The Quare Fellow</u> clearly <u>belongs</u> to
Irish drama, but <u>The Hostage</u> belongs to Joan Littlewood.

MacLiammoir, Michael. <u>Theatre in Ireland</u>. London, 1964.
　　The updated 1964 edition has added material
which treats Irish drama of the 1950s and comments
on <u>The Quare Fellow</u> and <u>The Hostage</u>.

MacMahon, Bryan. "Brendan Behan: Vital Human Being, A
Memoir." <u>North American Review</u>, 1 (Summer 1964),
60-64.
　　The author's friendship with Behan spanned two
decades. He affectionately recalls the playwright
as a witty and eloquent man who lost the battle of
drinking. The Irish people always forgave Brendan
his sins; they will miss him a long time.

Marcus, Steven. "Tom Brown in Quod." <u>Partisan Review</u>,
26 (Spring 1959), 335-44.
　　This is an article-review concentrating on
<u>Borstal Boy</u>. Marcus holds that, even though impris-
onment has been a major part of Behan's life, it is
wrong to compare him to a professional criminal-
turned-artist like Jean Genet, for Behan is much
less attuned to the anarchic spirit of the twentieth
century. Irish culture and history have permanently
connected him to tradition and the past.

Marowitz, Charles. "New Wave in Dead Sea." <u>X, A Quar-</u>
<u>terly Review</u>, 1 (4 October 1960), 270-77.
　　Marowitz includes Behan as a member of the "new
wave" movement in British drama. But Behan seems to
still be "preoccupied with the black-and-tan dilem-
mas of O'Casey."

Martin, Augustine. "Brendan Behan." _Threshold_, 18
(1963), 22-28.
    Martin discusses _The Quare Fellow_ and _The
Hostage_, making special note of the role of humor in
The Quare Fellow.

McCann, Sean, ed. _The World of Brendan Behan_. London:
New English Library, 1965.
    This is an uneven collection of articles on
Behan. Most fall under the heading of casual
reminiscence, but a few make important contributions
to Behan scholarship. Perhaps most interesting is
the reprint of Kiely's "That Old Triangle." Sullivan's "The Last Playboy of the Western World" is also one of the better pieces. Terry O'Sullivan's
article on Dublin pubs ("His Dublin Haunts") makes
an excellent companion to the innumerable accounts
of drinking tours available. Overviews of Behan's
career by John B. Keane and Michael MacLiammoir are
also of interest.

Mercier, Vivian. "The Dublin Tradition." _The New Repub-
lic_, 6 August 1956, pp. 21-22.
    This is a brief look at the various theatres
and repertory companies of Dublin, concentrating on
the history of Dublin drama. Behan's _The Quare Fel-
low_ is mentioned as a play "which some regard as the
most original Irish play for years."

Milne, Tom and Clive Goodwin. "Working with Joan." In
Theatre at Work. Eds. Charles Marowitz and Simon
Trussler. London: Methuen, 1967. Pp. 113-22.
    The authors talk with Theatre Workshop actors,
who describe the production of _The Quare Fellow_.

Muggeridge, Malcolm. "Brendan Behan at Lime Grove," _New
Statesman_, 27 March 1964, p. 488.
    Muggeridge recalls his famous TV interview with
Behan when Behan was too drunk to speak coherently.
Muggeridge calls the occasion "the pleasantest and
most rewarding evening I ever spent in Lime Grove."

Murphy, Brian. "Brendan Behan at Theatre Workshop: Story-
teller into Playwright." _Prompt_, 5 (1964), 4-8.
    Murphy has appeared in Theatre Workshop produc-
tions of both _The Quare Fellow_ and _The Hostage_. He
claims that the contribution of Littlewood and the
cast to _The Quare Fellow_ was negligible. In the
case of _The Hostage_, the play was changed consider-
ably during rehearsal, he admits, but he maintains
that many of the "improvised" lines came from Behan's talk. It remained Behan's play, according to
Murphy.

Nores, Dominique. "Reconnaissance de Brendan Behan."
    Lettres Nouvelles, October 1962, 132-37.

O'Brien, Conor Cruise. Writers and Politics. New York:
    Pantheon, 1965. Pp. 126-27.
    O'Brien comments briefly on Behan's attitude
    toward England and her prison system, as revealed
    by Borstal Boy.

O'Brien, Frank. "Another Revolution: Modern Poetry in
    Irish." Eire-Ireland, 1 (Winter 1966), 13-22.
    On the basis of his few Gaelic poems of the
    Forties and early Fifties, Behan is considered one
    of the major poets of his generation writing in
    Irish.

O'Brien, Kate. "Irish Genius." New Statesman, 27 March
    1964, p. 488.
    Behan is remembered as one of the giants of
    Irish literature and as a gentle man who was "gener-
    ous to [the point of] madness."

O'Connor, Patrick. Farrow, 15 (June 1964), 410-12.
    O'Connor compares Dylan Thomas and Behan, sees
    both as being free of literary affectation. Both
    had personalities which combined "savagery and
    generality." The Quare Fellow contains a documentary
    treatise on capital punishment but its "humanity and
    generosity" make it more. The Hostage is a "mod-
    ern morality."
    Behan lacks taste but has "instinctive sense of
    character, a quick ear for a phrase, an observing
    eye and an artist's sense of detachment. Above all
    he had heart."

O'Connor, Phillip. "Writing in Class." Antioch Review,
    19 (Summer 1959), 271-76.
    O'Connor maintains that English literature is
    rather sharply divided between mass entertainment
    and "contemporary exposition of traditional culture";
    there are faint symptoms of fusion of the two sides
    in the work of Behan, Frank Norman, and Bill Naugh-
    ton.

O'Connor, Ulick. Brendan Behan. London: Hamish Hamil-
    ton, 1970.
    As the first full-blown biography of Behan,
    this is one of the most important works of Behan
    scholarship to appear. Careful and well-written,
    it provides details of the life previously unre-
    vealed, particularly those concerning the Paris
    period of the Forties. Unfortunately, the book has
    been widely criticized for inaccuracies and for
    O'Connor's flat assertion that Behan was bisexual.

It remains, however, the fullest statement yet on
Behan's life.

O'hAodha, Michael. Theatre in Ireland. Totowa, N.J.:
Rowman and Littlefield, 1974. Pp. 143-48.
    O'hAodha comments not only on The Quare Fellow,
The Hostage, and Borstal Boy, but also on some of
the lesser works: "Confirmation Suit," three radio
plays (Moving Out, A Garden Party, and The Big
House) and Richard's Cork Leg.

O'Kelly, Seamus G. "I Knew the Real Brendan Behan."
Irish Digest, 80 (June 1964), 67-70.
    O'Kelly looks at Behan's politics and concludes
that no one can understand him without taking his
Republicanism into account.

O'Neill, John Drew. "Brendan Go Bragh!" Michigan Quarterly Review, 4 (Winter 1965), 19-22.
    Behan's death is seen as a great loss to the
theatre. His view of life was sane and clear. He
is called the "authentic voice of the Irish under-
ground."

O'Reilly, Michael. "Brendan--The Human Behan." Irish
Digest, 77 (May 1963), 15-18.
    O'Reilly reports that Behan has not been made
happy by success. He is quoted, saying: "My one
ambition is to live as long as I can."

Osamu, Osaka "Critical Notes on Brendan Behan--with
Special Reference to His Plays." Studies in English
Literature and Language (Kyushu Univ., Fukuoka,
Japan), 24, 79-104. (In Japanese.)

_____. "Critical Notes on Brendan Behan (2): The
Making of The Quare Fellow and Its Analysis."
Studies in English Literature and Language, 25, 45-
79. (In Japanese.)

Phelps, Corey. "Borstal Revisited." ICarbS, 2 (1975),
39-60.
    Phelps analyzes three early fragments of Bor-
stal Boy in the Morris Library in Southern Illinois
University. He compares the language, style, and
subject matter of these early typescripts and concludes that Behan was the victim of poor editorial
advice and/or censorship. He finds the original
versions generally superior. This is a valuable
study not only of the genesis of Borstal Boy but
also of Behan's mode of creation.

Porter, Raymond. Brendan Behan. New York: Columbia
    University Press, 1973.
        This is a very brief introduction to Behan's
    works.

Preger, Janie. "Brendan." Guardian, 6 March 1965, p. 5.
        Preger knew Brendan when she was a child. She
    remembers him as a very kind, generous, and apolo-
    getic drunk.

"Problems that Confront the New Abbey Theatre." Irish
    Digest, 78 (October 1963), 79-82.
        Behan, among other major Irish playwrights, has
    had little connection with the Abbey Theatre. It
    should attempt to draw out such talents.

Rafroidi, Patrick. "Plays for Ireland." In Aspects of
    the Irish Theatre. Eds. Patrick Rafroidi, Raymonde
    Popot and William Parker. Lille, France: L'Univer-
    site de Lille, 1972. Pp. 67-74.
        See Keane bibliography below.

Robbins, Jhan and June. "Beatrice and Brendan Behan:
    Love Remembered." Redbook, March 1966, pp. 60-63.
        The often stormy and finally tragic love affair
    of the Brendan Behans is remembered.

Robinson, Liam. "The Great Adventure of Merry Mrs.
    Behan." Irish Digest, 77 (November 1962), 15-18.
        Mrs. Behan comments on an autobiography she is
    in the process of writing. She speaks of his hatred
    of police, his fondness for children, his drinking
    problem, his love of the underdog.

Russell, F. "Dublin in the Doldrums." National Review,
    14 July 1964, p. 612.
        The effect Behan's death has had on Dublin is
    described.

Ryan, Stephen P. "Crisis in Irish Letters; Literary Life
    in Dublin." The Commonwealth, 18 December 1959,
    pp. 347-49.
        The author describes the current situation in
    Irish letters: fiction, criticism, drama. Behan
    is mentioned briefly as "the sort of literary 'char-
    acter' who yarns up in Dublin at regular intervals,
    just as things are getting a bit dull." Ryan does
    not hold out any hope that Behan or any other cur-
    rent playwright is a worthy successor to those of
    the Irish Renaissance.

_____. "Ireland and Its Writers." Catholic World,
    1149 (December 1960), 149-55.
        Since the establishment of the Irish Free State,

many Irish writers have emigrated but continue their
complaints against the Church and the sterility of
Irish society. Behan is discussed in this context
along with Frank O'Connor and Brian Moore. Ryan
feels that upon leaving Ireland writers seem to
lose some of their language skills.

Sieradzka-Gryminska, Teresa. "Brendan Behan's Confes-
sions of an Irish Rebel: A Sample of Anglo-Irish
Novelized Autobiography." Zagadnienia Rodzajow
Literaskich (Poland), 17 (1974), 50-64.
    This article only peripherally touches on the
plays but is interesting as a continental view of
Behan's work.

Simpson, Alan. Beckett and Behan and a Theatre in Dublin.
London: Routledge and Kegan Paul, 1962.
    This contains a short biography of Behan up to
his last years and a history of the first production
of The Quare Fellow.

_____. "Introduction" to Behan's Richard's Cork Leg.
London: Eyre Methuen, 1973. Pp. 5-11.
    Simpson briefly sketches his long relationship
with Brendan and describes the editing of the frag-
ments which comprise Richard's Cork Leg.

Smith, Paul. "Dublin's Lusty Theatre." Holiday, 33
(April 1963), 119.
    This is a history of the Irish theatre with at-
tention paid largely to the main theatres--the
Abbey, the Gate--and to personalities such as
Michael MacLiammoir and Lord Longford. Behan is the
only really contemporary playwright discussed--for
two paragraphs. He is described as a "playwright
very much of the Dublin scene today, but of neither
literary nor any real theatrical importance. . . ."

Styan, J. L. "The Published Play after 1956." British
Book News: A Guide to Book Selection, 300 (August
1965), 521-25.
    Recent British drama is seen as rebellious.
John Osborne and Behan are the dramatists who have
been most successful in fusing protest themes with
new dramatic techniques.

Sullivan, A. M. "In Durance Vile--and Later." Saturday
Review, 28 February 1959, p. 35.
    Sullivan looks at Borstal Boy and praises
Behan's insight into the lower level of humanity,
but takes exception to the playwright's vocabulary,
finding the profanity "more tiresome than offensive"
and the slang a "thorny path for the stranger."

Sullivan, Kevin. "Last Playboy of the Western World."
    Nation, 15 March 1965, pp. 283-87. (Reprinted in
    McCann's The World of Brendan Behan.)
        Sullivan says that only Behan's early works are
    worthwhile. In these his most engaging quality is
    that "he takes such obvious, and so highly communi-
    cable a joy in what he is doing."

Sutton, Horace. "Recalling the Borstal Boy." Saturday
    Review, 2 December 1967, pp. 48-49.
        Travel writer Sutton tours Brendan's Dublin,
    taking in pubs such as McDaid's, the White Horse,
    John Mulligan's, and--from Ulysses--Davy Byrnes' and
    the Bailey.

Swann, C. "There's No Place on Earth like the World!"
    Theatre Arts, 46 (November 1962), 26-27.
        Swann traces the history of The Hostage's first
    production in the U.S. It reveals Behan's essential
    warmth and humor.

"Tippler on Television." Newsweek, 2 July 1956, p. 70.
        This is a contemporary account of Behan's
    famous drunken interview with Malcolm Muggeridge.
    The show drew, among other things, a formal protest
    from the Church of England Temperance Society and
    this defense from Behan: "Of course I was drunk.
    You don't think anyone could appear sober on tele-
    vision?"

Taylor, John Russell. Anger and After. London: Methuen,
    1962. Pp. 102-08. (Published in the U.S. under the
    title The Angry Theatre.)
        Taylor discusses The Quare Fellow and The Hos-
    tage, concluding that the former is much the supe-
    rior. He thinks The Hostage "sometimes looked in
    danger of drowning in a sea of words," but that The
    Quare Fellow is "something very like a masterpiece."

Trilling, Ossia. "The New English Realism." Tulane
    Drama Review, 7 (Winter 1962), 184-93.
        Behan is seen as one of the leaders in the
    "tide of revolt" in contemporary British drama. This
    began with Osborne's Look Back in Anger. The new
    realism has two elements: resistance to British
    class structure and the universal world dilemma of
    potential nuclear destruction. Older writers like
    Christopher Fry and John Whiting join new ones like
    Behan, Pinter, and Delaney in this revolt.

Tynan, Kenneth. A View of the English Stage: 1944-63.
    London: Davis Poynter, 1975. Pp. 179-80, 225-28.
        Tynan includes his reviews of The Quare Fellow
    and The Hostage. He applauds the language of

the former and calls the latter an example of "Com-
media dell 'Arte." "It is Ireland's sacred duty"--
he says--"to send over, every few years, a playwright to save the English theatre from inarticulate
glumness."

Walker, James Robert. "Irisches Zeugnis: Brendan Behan."
    Merkur, 18 (July 1964), 691-96. (In German.)

Wall, Richard. "An Giall and The Hostage Compared."
    Modern Drama, 18 (June 1975), 165-72.
        Wall finds that The Hostage is much more than a
    mere translation of An Giall; it amounts to a major
    revision. It contains Irish jigs, wild drinking,
    anti-English rebel songs, mob scenes, etc., which
    are not in the Irish version. It was Behan's aim to
    make the play more understandable and appealing to
    an English audience, but he succeeded only in de-
    stroying its integrity and drastically altering its
    tone.

Weintraub, Stanley. "To Dublin in a Donkey Cart."
    Saturday Review, 4 June 1966, p. 47.
        This is a double review of Dominic Behan's My
    Brother Brendan and Brendan's own Confessions of an
    Irish Rebel. Weintraub dislikes the first on the
    whole (wondering how well Dominic really knew his
    brother) and approves of the latter, calling it:
    "Brendan Behan at his most flavorsome." It is a
    rare approval for this "taped" book.

Wellwarth, G. E. The Theatre of Protest and Paradox.
    New York: New York University Press, 1964. Pp. 303-06.
        Wellwarth discusses both The Quare Fellow and
    The Hostage and lists Behan among the traditional-
    ists of the new English dramatists.

Wickstrom, Gordon M. "The Heroic Dimension in Brendan
    Behan's The Hostage." Educational Theatre Journal,
    22 (1970), 406-11.
        Wickstrom's thesis is that Leslie, the soldier
    in The Hostage, is a heroic figure standing for
    "simple justice, love, and life." The play is essen-
    tially life-affirming; Leslie's revival at the end
    has mythical significance. He "returns in Pentecos-
    tal triumph, declaring himself and bestowing his
    blessing. . . ."

Wilson, Angus. "New Playwrights." Partisan Review, 26
    (Fall 1959), 631-34.
        Wilson reviews plays by Delaney, Doris Lessing,
    Bernard Kops, and Arnold Wesker which exemplify the
    burgeoning English stage. Behan is mentioned as a
    more famous representative of the same movement.

II. DISSERTATIONS

Capurso, Maria Antonietta. "Brendan Behan: Borstal Boy." Universita de Bari, Italy, 1975.

Gryminska, Teresa Sieradzka. "Contemporary Anglo-Irish Novelised Autobiography." University of Warsaw, 1973.

Harsch, J. H. "The Curtain of Words: Dualism in the Plays of Synge, O'Casey, Johnston, Behan and Beckett." University of Dublin, 1971.

Lanoix, Louis. "Le theatre de Brendan Behan." Sorbonne, Paris, 1965.

Lauffet, Lisette. "Realism and Poetry in the Works of Brendan Behan." University of Strasbourg, 1968.

Moncada, Angelo. "An Approach to Brendan Behan." Universita degli studi di Venezia, 1972/73.

Pannecoucke, Jean-Michel. "Music and Drama: O'Casey, Behan, Keane." L'Université de Lille, 1970.

Pierrotin, Jean-Pierre. "Brendan Behan." University of Strasbourg, 1968.

III. REVIEWS

THE BIG HOUSE

The Times, 30 July 1963, p. 13.

BORSTAL BOY

The Times, 30 October 1958, p. 13.

New York Times, 22 February 1959, VII:1.

Newsweek, 23 February 1959, pp. 106-06.

New York Times, 27 February 1959, p. 23.

Nation, 28 February 1959, pp. 190-91.

Saturday Night, 28 February 1959, pp. 27-28.

Time, 9 March 1959, pp. 86-87.

Commonweal, 13 March 1959, pp. 628-29.

New Yorker, 4 July 1959, pp. 69-72.

Ariel, 7 (April 1976), 47-62.

BORSTAL BOY (play)

New Yorker, 11 April 1970, pp. 81-82.

Newsweek, 13 April 1970, p. 83.

Time, 13 April 1970, p. 57.

Saturday Review, 18 April 1970, p. 26.

Nation, 20 April 1970, p. 473.

America, 2 May 1970, p. 483.

Life, 22 May 1970, p. 16.

BRENDAN BEHAN'S ISLAND

The Times, 5 October 1962, p. 17.

New York Times, 23 October 1962, p. 35.

New York Times, 4 November 1962, VII:5.

Reporter, 31 January 1963, p. 56.

BRENDAN BEHAN'S NEW YORK

New York Times, 19 November 1964, VII:6.

CONFESSIONS OF AN IRISH REBEL

Nation, 7 November 1966, pp. 486-88.

HOLD YOUR HOUR AND HAVE ANOTHER

The Times, 26 September 1963, p. 15.

New York Times, 28 January 1964, p. 29.

New York Times, 2 February 1964, VII:7.

THE HOSTAGE

The Times, 15 October 1958, p. 8.

Educational Theatre Journal, II (March 1959), 19-39.

The Times, 6 April 1959, p. 3.

Le Figaro Litteraire, 11 April 1959, p. 16.
    Critic Jacques Le Marchand focuses on the
comic aspects of The Hostage and maintains that
the "youthfulness, generosity, and comedy . . .
endow this treatment of a study of our time
with a novelty and liberty which make it ex-
tremely provocative."

New Yorker, 18 April 1959, p. 156.

Studies: An Irish Quarterly, 48 (Spring 1959), 111-
    113.
    Playwright and critic Thomas Kilroy be-
lieves Behan has brought new life to the Irish
stage, has fused traditional themes with new
ideas and techniques.

The Times, 12 June 1959, p. 15.

New York Times, 21 September 1960, p. 42.

The Times, 22 September 1960, p. 16.

New Yorker, 1 October 1960, p. 128.

New Republic, 3 October 1960, pp. 20-21.

Newsweek, 3 October 1960, p. 57.

Nation, 8 October 1960, p. 236.

Saturday Review, 8 October 1960, p. 32.

New York Times, 11 October 1960, p. 50.

America, 22 October 1960, p. 130.

Catholic World, 192 (November 1960), 126-27.

Reporter, 24 November 1960, p. 45.

Hudson Review, 13 (Winter 1960-61), 587-88.

Horizon, 3 (January 1961), 113-14.

The Times, 14 February 1961, p. 6.

Educational Theatre Journal, 13 (March 1961), 46-56.

Sewanee Review, 69 (Spring 1961), 335-37.

New Yorker, 23 December 1961, pp. 57-58.

Commonweal, 5 January 1962, p. 389.

Saturday Review, 19 May 1962, p. 30.

The Times, 1 October 1964, p. 15.

New York Times, 12 May 1972, p. 24.

New Yorker, 21 October 1972, p. 56.

Nation, 30 October 1972, pp. 410-11.

IRISH FOLK SONGS AND BALLADS (recording)

Saturday Review, 12 March 1960, p. 84.

THE QUARE FELLOW

   Dublin Magazine, n.s. 31 (January-March 1955), 47-49.
           Critic A. J. Leventhal finds The Quare
   Fellow has "no recognizable form" but considers
   it a "powerful piece of propaganda." He praises
   the Pike Theatre for producing the play and
   comments on Behan's "rich Dublin modern slang
   laced with a specialized lay lingo."

   The Times, 25 May 1956, p. 3.
           The Quare Fellow is called a "powerful
   portrait of life in prison." Though maintaining that Behan's wholesale inclusion of so many
   raucous comedians tends to get in the way of
   the play's action, the reviewer praises it
   highly. He quotes from Behan's curtain call
   speech: "Miss Littlewood's company have performed a better play than I wrote."

   The Times, 25 July 1956, p. 5.

   Irish Writing, 36 (Autumn-Winter 1956-57), 189-90.

   Dublin Magazine, 32 (1957), 52-53.

   Time, 29 July 1957, p. 82.

   New York Times, 28 November 1958, p. 34.

   New Yorker, 6 December 1958, pp. 119-20.

   Newsweek, 8 December 1958, pp. 69-70.

   Time, 8 December 1958, p. 78.

   Saturday Review, 13 December 1958, pp. 27-28.

   Vogue, 1 January 1959, p. 66.

Commonweal, 23 January 1959, pp. 438-49.

Catholic World, 188 (February 1959), 420.

Theatre Arts, 43 (February 1959), 66.

Die Welt, 17 March 1959, p. 16.
Friedrich Luft, reviewing the German
première of The Quare Fellow, says, "this is a
report of a flop, the notification of a complete artistic washout."

The Times, 5 October 1962, p. 18.

THE SCARPERER

Saturday Review, 20 June 1964, p. 36.

New York Times, 21 June 1964, VII:5.

New York Times, 23 June 1964, p. 31.

Hudson Review, 17 (Autumn 1964), 470-77.

John Boyd

Born in Belfast, n.d.

John Boyd has written powerful dramas about modern
political and social complexities for more than twenty
years. His specific scene is troubled Northern Ireland
in recent times, but his themes are universal. To what
extent is man a victim of changing political philosophies,
religious and ethnic prejudice? When do peace-loving
citizens feel they must become involved in factional
strife? All of these questions are addressed in Boyd's
The Flats, a painful and moving study of everyday people
caught in the horrors of civil war. Boyd was also on the
staff of the B.B.C. for many years and created radio
dramas containing the same suspenseful probing of moral
and political issues which characterize his stage plays.
He remains in Belfast where he is currently concluding
work on The Protestants.

PRIMARY SOURCES

I. STAGE

The Assassin. (A rewritten version of The Blood of
      Colonel Lamb.) Staged Dublin, 1969.

The Blood of Colonel Lamb. Staged Belfast, 1967.

The Farm. Staged Belfast, 1972.

The Flats. Staged Belfast, 1971; New York, 1972;
      Lawrence, Kansas, 1972. Belfast: Blackstaff Press,
      1974.

Guests. Staged Belfast, 1974.

<u>Mrs</u>. <u>Martin's</u> <u>Man</u>. Staged Belfast, 1956.

<u>The</u> <u>Protestants</u>. Staged Belfast, 1978.

<u>Speranza's</u> <u>Boy</u> (on the life of Oscar Wilde). Staged
     Belfast, 1978.

<u>The</u> <u>Street</u>. Staged Belfast, 1976.

II. RADIO   (Until 30 September 1967, B.B.C. transmitted
             three services: Light Programs [LP], Third
             Programs [TP], and Home Service [NIHS].
             After this time these channels were known
             as B.B.C. 2, 3, and 4 respectively.)

<u>All</u> <u>Fall</u> <u>Down</u>, 13 September 1965, NIHS.

<u>The</u> <u>Assassin</u>, 8 October 1969, B.B.C. 4.

<u>Evening</u> <u>with</u> <u>a</u> <u>Gunman</u>, 17 September 1963, NIHS.

<u>The</u> <u>Flats</u>, 26 January 1971, B.B.C. 4.

<u>Strictly</u> <u>Private</u>, 7 April 1964, NIHS.

III. FICTION

"The Air-Gun." <u>Threshold</u>, no. 20 (Winter 1966-67),
     5-21.

IV. NONFICTION

"The Achievement of Forrest Read." <u>Dublin</u> <u>Magazine</u>,
     n.s., 20 (July-September 1945), <u>18-24</u>.

"Wordsworth's Irish Town." <u>Dublin</u> <u>Magazine</u>, n.s., 19
     (July-September 1944), <u>29-34</u>.

V. POETRY

"Visit to a School." <u>Rann</u>, 1 (Summer 1948), n.p.

SECONDARY SOURCES

I. CRITICISM

Bell, Sam Hanna. The Theatre in Ulster. Totowa, N.J.:
    Rowman and Littlefield, 1972. Pp. 101-02.
        Bell comments favorably on Boyd's documentary
    style. He provides a brief survey of the play-
    wright's achievements and discusses the popularity
    and impact of The Flats.

Bertram, James. "The Watchers." Landfall, 13 (March
    1959), 90-92.
        Although Bertram is primarily concerned with
    Boyd's reputation as a poet, it is worth noting
    that Bertram considers him "a romantic" philosophi-
    cally and praises his use of language which is
    "genuinely haunted by his angels."

Foster, John Wilson. Forces and Themes in Ulster Fic-
    tion. Totowa, N.J.: Rowman and Littlefield, 1974.
    Pp. 29, 131, 139.
        Foster alludes to Boyd's work as a critic in
    "The Arts in Ulster" on several occasions.

Hogan, Robert, Bonnie K. Scott and Gordon Henderson.
    "The Modern Drama." In Anglo-Irish Literature: A
    Review of Research. Ed. Richard J. Finneran. New
    York: Modern Language Association, 1976. P. 559.
        Boyd is one of the most prominent Northern
    Irish dramatists and one of the few to draw directly
    on the political turbulence in Belfast.

Maxwell, D. E. S. "Imagining the North: Violence and
    the Writers." Eire-Ireland, 8 (Summer 1973), 91-
    107.
        Boyd is one of a number of authors discussed
    who have dealt with the violence in Northern Ire-
    land. None of these writers has exhibited partisan-
    ship, but Boyd has revealed an impressive under-
    standing of Irish political complexities and of the
    personal trauma the Irish are experiencing.

Rushe, Desmond. "Theatre: Brave Tokens." Eire-Ireland,
    9 (February 1976), 106-109.
        Boyd's The Assassin and The Flats and Friel's
    The Freedom of the City are discussed as convincing
    examples that effective drama has resulted from the
    political conflicts in North Ireland. Rushe regret-
    tably insists on comparing the two writers unfavor-
    ably with O'Casey.

II. REVIEWS

THE ASSASSIN

> Wardle, Irving. "A Dublin View of Swift," The
> Times, 6 October 1969, p. 13.
>   A discussion of the current Dublin festi-
> val and two biographical plays, Eugene McCabe's
> Swift and John Boyd's The Assassin. "A radio
> feature writ large," the latter follows a
> series of flashback episodes charting the life
> of Col. Luther Lamb who is shot by a Civil
> Rights worker in the first scene. Wardle com-
> ments that "it is a well graded performance
> with more irony and comedy than the play prom-
> ises at the outset."

> Hughes, Catherine. "Theatre in Dublin." Nation,
> 24 November 1969, pp. 579-80.
>   Commencing with a generally negative
> evaluation of the 1969 Dublin Theater Festival,
> which Hughes claims is more "adventurous polit-
> ically than it was successful artistically,"
> she goes on to cite John Boyd's controversial
> radical revision of The Assassin performed in
> Belfast earlier. "Free Doherty" handbills
> underlined the political sentiment which colors
> this story of the assassination of demagogic
> Protestant Rev. Luther Lamb (a pale covering
> for obvious Ian Paisley identification). De-
> spite "considerable theatricality" Hughes be-
> lieves that characters are not fleshed out and
> that a real play on the subject can be more
> easily found "in the faces one sees in Bogside
> or Shonkill Road" in Belfast. [Also mentioned
> are Conor Cruise O'Brien's King Herod Explains,
> Eugene McCabe's Swift, and Hugh Leonard's The
> Barracks.]

THE FLATS

> The Times, 19 March 1971, p. 20.
>   Set in Belfast's Catholic Unity Flats this
> play is characterized as "objective and com-
> passionate" by its author. Boyd comments that
> he hopes "it will persuade the various factions
> to see the other side's viewpoint; that Catho-
> lics in the audience may understand the British
> soldiers a little better. . . ."

James Douglas

Born July 4, 1929, Bray, Co. Wicklow.

James Douglas attended the National School in Bray until he was fifteen years old and then transferred to a technical school to complete his formal education. For five years he was an apprentice electrician and continued to work as an electrician even after he began writing successful plays. He writes of anachronisms and lingering puritanical attitudes in modern Irish life. More than other recent Irish playwrights he deals with contemporary man's basic alienation and loneliness. Failed attempts at communication in his plays create a terse, almost elliptical dialogue and occasionally remind his audiences of techniques associated with Pinter, Arden, or Bond. There is an awareness of violence in Douglas's world, but the central emphasis of his plays is on everyday responses to varieties of stress and frustration. He relies heavily on symbols and stylized fragmentary scenes which are often underscored with a subtext of psychological game-playing. His Collected Plays will soon be published by Proscenium Press.

PRIMARY SOURCES

I. STAGE

Carrie, A Musical. Staged Dublin, 1963.

The Ice Goddess. Staged Dublin, 1964.

_____. In Seven Irish Plays. Ed. Robert Hogan. Minneapolis: University of Minnesota Press, 1967.

North City Traffic Straight Ahead. Staged Dublin, 1961.

_____. Dixon, Ca.: Proscenium Press, 1968.

The Savages. Staged Dublin, 1967.

II. TELEVISION (produced by Telefis Éireann)

The Bomb, 1964.

_____. Dixon, Ca.: Proscenium Press, 1966.

The Hollow Field, 1965.

How Long Is Kissing Time?, 1965.

The Riordans (a serial), 1965.

III. RADIO (B.B.C. Radio 4)

The Eels in the Ranny Are Dead, 10 March 1971.

Babby Joe, 30 October 1968.

Adman's Gothic, 23 May 1975.

IV. FICTION

"Adman's Gothic." Journal of Irish Literature, 1 (1973),
    3-23.

"P.J." The Kilkenny Magazine, no. 5 (Autumn-Winter
    1961), 30-33.

"Son." The Bell, 17 (February 1963), 568-72.

SECONDARY SOURCES

I. CRITICISM

Hogan, Robert. After the Irish Renaissance: A Critical
    History of the Irish Drama Since The Plough and
    the Stars. Minneapolis: University of Minnesota
    Press, 1967. Pp. 192-95.
        In contrast to that of Keane, Douglas's work is
    "urban and modern." North City Traffic Straight Ahead
    reveals the influence of Sherwood Anderson's Wines-
    burg, Ohio. Its hero, Harry Hopkins, is seen as a
    middle-aged Jimmy Porter. The Ice Goddess is also

discussed. Hogan sees Douglas as being midway between realism and absurdism in the theatre, like
England's John Arden.

_____. "Where Have All the Shamrocks Gone?" In As-
pects of the Irish Theatre. Eds. Patrick Rafroidi,
Raymonde Popot and William Parker. Lille: L'Université de Lille, 1972. Pp. 261-71.
    Douglas interests Hogan because he is primarily
a modern, rather than an Irish, playwright. Douglas's themes are isolation and loneliness in the
modern world, the death of idealism, and changing
value systems. North City Traffic Straight Ahead,
The Ice Goddess, and The Savages are among the plays
dicussed.

_____, Bonnie K. Scott and Gordon Henderson. "The
Modern Drama." In Anglo-Irish Literature: A Review
of Research. Ed. Richard J. Finneran. New York:
Modern Language Association, 1976. P. 552.
    Douglas's career is briefly summarized and his
emphasis on the modern, urban scene is noted.

Kenny, Herbert A. Literary Dublin: A History. Dublin:
    Gill and MacMillan, 1974. P. 283.
    Douglas is cited for his fine television
achievements and successful work in the theatre.

Mercier, Vivian. "Foreword." Aspects of the Irish
    Theatre. Eds. Patrick Rafroidi, Raymonde Popot
    and William Parker. Lille: L'Université de Lille,
    1972.
    Mercier briefly compares plays by Douglas to
those of Albee and Tennessee Williams.

II. REVIEWS

CARRIE

    The Times, 9 October 1963, p. 166.
            The reviewer notes that "audience-wise
        Carrie was the success of the festival (Dub-
        lin)." The play's music by Michael Coffee
        was "pleasant with some attractive songs"--
        "Maybe I'm Just a Fool," "Love's a Thing of
        the Past." The excellent dancing, however,
        could not entirely compensate for the somewhat
        weak characterization and occasionally unevent-
        ful plot.

41

THE ICE GODDESS

"A Dublin Given Over to Plays." The Times, 28 September 1964, p. 14.

Beginning with an overview of the Dublin art festival, this reviewer concentrates on "the week's most uncompromising show," James Douglas's new play about a boy's fantasy life in a tree cabin. With no explicitly national themes the play builds on "meticulously poised dialogue" and scenes which "chill the atmosphere." The feud between the boy's grandmother and her son-in-law, who has gone into coffin-making to save the family fortunes, emphasizes the dramatist's obsession with property.

NORTH CITY TRAFFIC STRAIGHT AHEAD

The Times, 21 September 1961, p. 16.

Simpson's production is "a play of mood," showing O'Neill's influence on Douglas. "The city traffic rolls on indifferently while the private tragedies and frustrations of the characters come to no clear conclusion, much like life," writes this reviewer. Intellectuals like the play; ordinary theatregoers do not.

Brian Friel

Born January 5, 1929, Omagh, Co. Tyrone.

Of the living playwrights in this volume Brian Friel
is, perhaps, the best known outside of Ireland. Philadelphia, Here I Come! had highly successful runs in New
York and London and is the work most closely identified
with Friel in the public imagination. He is also a
highly successful short story writer. Friel describes
lonely, inhibited people trapped in a chilling puritanical society, but his humorous dialogue and clever staging
make his drama entertaining. There is an alarming darkness at the center of his work, however, which seems to
be growing stronger. Not overly polemical, he is none-
theless sensitive to the divisiveness in modern society,
and as a Northern Catholic writer, he has been deeply
touched by recent political conflicts. Friel's innova-
tive theatrical methods have given way to an increasing
simplicity, but his characters continue to be authentic,
recognizable, and compassionately drawn.

PRIMARY SOURCES

I. STAGE

The Blind Mice. Staged Dublin, 1963.

Crystal and Fox. Staged Dublin, 1968; Los Angeles, 1970;
    New York, 1973. London: Faber and Faber, 1970.

_____. In Two Plays: Crystal and Fox and The Mundy
    Scheme. New York: Farrar Straus, 1970.

The Enemy Within. Staged Dublin, 1962. Journal of Irish
    Literature, 4 (May 1975), 3-64.

_____. Vol 7. The Irish Play Series. Newark, Delaware: Proscenium Press, 1975.

Faith Healer. Staged New York, 1976.

The Francophile. Staged Belfast, 1960. Later called A Doubtful Paradise.

The Freedom of the City. Staged Dublin, London, and Chicago, 1973; New York, 1974. London: Faber and Faber, 1974.

_____. In The Critic, 32, no. 1, n.d., 38-72.

The Gentle Island. Staged Dublin, 1971. London: Davis Poynter, 1973.

Lovers: Part One: Winners; Part Two: Losers. Staged Dublin, 1967; New York, 1968; London, 1969. New York: Farrar Straus, 1968.

_____. London: Faber and Faber, 1969.

The Loves of Cass McGuire. Staged New York, 1966; Dublin, 1967; London, 1970. London: Faber and Faber, 1967.

_____. New York: Farrar Straus, 1967.

The Mundy Scheme. Staged Dublin and New York, 1969. In Two Plays: Crystal and Fox and The Mundy Scheme. New York: Farrar Straus, 1970.

Philadelphia, Here I Come! Staged Dublin, 1964; New York, 1966; London, 1967. London: Faber and Faber, 1965.

_____. New York: Farrar Straus, 1966.

Volunteers. Staged Dublin, 1975.

II. RADIO (See note on Boyd's radio plays, p. 36.)

The Founder Members, 9 March 1964, LP.

The Loves of Cass McGuire, 9 August 1966, TP.

A Sort of Freedom, 16 January 1958, NIHS.

To This Hard House, 24 April 1958, NIHS.

Winners, 14 April 1968, TP.

III. FILM

Philadelphia, Here I Come! 1970.

IV. FICTION

"Among the Ruins." Threshold, no. 2 (Summer 1967), 117-
28.

"The Child." The Bell, 18 (July 1952), 232-33.

The Gold in the Sea. London: Gollancz, and New York:
Doubleday, 1966.

The Saucer of Larks. London: Gollancz, and New York:
Doubleday, 1962.

"The Visitation." Kilkenny Magazine, no. 5 (Autumn-Winter 1961-62), 8-14.

V. NONFICTION

"Self-Portrait." Aquarius, 5 (1973), 17-22.

"Sex in Ireland (Republic of)." The Critic, 30 (1973),
20-21.

"A Visit to Spain." Irish Monthly, 80 (November 1952),
342-44.

VI. TRANSLATIONS

PHILADELPHIA, HERE I COME!

Ver Elini, Yeni Dünya. Tr. by Asade Zeybekoglu.
Istanbul: Kagit ve Basim Isleri A. S., 1966.
Turkish.

THE GOLD IN THE SEA. THE SAUCER OF LARKS.

Das Strohwitwen-System: Erzählungen. Tr. by Elisabeth Schnack. Zürich: Diogenes-Verlag, 1970.

Das Strohwitwen-System: Erzählungen. Tr. by Elisabeth Schnack. Munich: König, 1973. German.

VII. INTERVIEW

"Brian Friel interviewed by G. Morison." Acorn, no. 8
    (Spring 1965), n.p.
        Friel protests against the use of the theatre
    as a political forum in the works of Osborne or
    Wesker. He believes everyone should be concerned
    with his society, but a writer must report from the
    sidelines to maintain objectivity and balance. His
    own job is to present "a set of people and a situa-
    tion with clarity and understanding and sympathy,
    and as a result of this we should look at them more
    closely; and if one is moved then, that one should
    react accordingly. This is the responsibility of
    the reader or an audience, but I don't think it's
    the writer's."

SECONDARY SOURCES

I. CRITICISM

Bell, Sam Hanna. The Theatre in Ulster. Totowa, N.J.:
    Rowman and Littlefield, 1972. P. 102.
        Bell believes one interpretation of The Enemy
    Within is that the "enemy is the thorn of prickly
    pride forever pricking the flesh of the man of God."

Bigsby, C. W. E. "Brian Friel." In Contemporary Drama.
    London: St. James Press, 1977. Pp. 275-77.
        Bigsby considers Friel Ireland's major drama-
    tist (excluding Beckett) and provides a summary of
    his career and a useful bibliography. He places
    him in the naturalist tradition and applauds his
    knowledge of stagecraft. Friel's plays are not
    political but have become increasingly dark and
    ironical.

Brady, Seamus. "Are They Our Great Writers of Tomorrow?"
    Irish Digest, 79 (November 1963), 9-12.
        Though the great writers of the Irish Renais-
    sance are either dead or in exile, there are five
    successors who deserve mention as battlers against
    the pervasive materialism of their times. Friel is
    included as one of the five, along with John McGa-
    hern, novelist; Richard Murphy, poet; John B. Keane
    and John O'Donovan, playwrights.

"Brian Friel: Derry's Playwright." Hibernia, n.v. (Feb-
    ruary 1975), 5.

Browne, Joseph. "Violent Prophecies: The Writer and
    Northern Ireland." Eire-Ireland, 10 (Summer 1975),
    109-19.
        The works of Friel and Behan--among many other
    Irish writers--reveal their accurate predictions of
    violence in Ireland.

Coakley, James. "Chekhov in Ireland: Brief Notes on
    Friel's Philadelphia." Comparative Drama, 7 (Fall
    1973), 191-97.
        Coakley sees resemblances in the frustrations
    of Friel's hero, Gar, and the trapped, isolated
    characters of The Three Sisters and other Chekhovian
    dramas.

Encyclopedia of Ireland. Dublin: Allen Figgis, 1968.
    P. 328.
        This contains a brief survey of Friel's titles
    to date and notes his contribution to popular drama.

Fallis, Richard. The Irish Renaissance. Syracuse:
    Syracuse University Press, 1977. Pp. 271-74.
        Friel as a playwright from Ulster sometimes
    "portrays the divided self inherent in that schizo-
    phrenic province." Many of his plays seem like
    "staged short stories with an overlay of theatrical
    experience." Friel's many achievements are sur-
    veyed, however, and Fallis considers him an impres-
    sive Irish literary figure.

Foster, John Wilson. Forces and Themes in Ulster Fiction.
    Totowa, N.J.: Rowman and Littlefield, 1974. Pp. 64-
    72.
        This generally favorable evaluation of Friel's
    work emphasizes the connection between his charac-
    ters' poverty and their need to fantasize. He pri-
    marily focuses on Friel's short fiction such as
    "The Widowhood System" and "Foundry House" but com-
    ments on the failure of Philadelphia, Here I Come!
    to offer "vibrating insight."

Hogan, Robert. After the Irish Renaissance: A Critical
    History of the Irish Drama Since The Plough and the
    Stars. Minneapolis: University of Minnesota Press,
    1967. Pp. 195-97.
        Hogan analyzes Philadelphia, Here I Come!, com-
    menting on Friel's brilliant device of dividing his
    hero into public and private selves. The play's
    theme is the failure of the Irish characters to com-
    municate their true feelings and wishes.

_____. "Dublin: The Summer Season and the Theatre
    Festival, 1967." Drama Survey, 6 (Spring 1968),

315-23.
Hogan discusses Dublin's 1967 Summer Season
and the Theatre Festival of that year. He thinks
that the best of the "straight plays" of the summer
was Brian Friel's Lovers. A synopsis of the play
is given. Friel's The Loves of Cass McGuire is
also discussed, as is Hugh Leonard's The Quick and
the Dead. Hogan describes the plot of the latter
and gives a list of what he considers Leonard's
best plays. Also discussed is Frank McMahon's
adaptation of Behan's Borstal Boy, the "most successful long play" of the season.

_____. "Where Have All the Shamrocks Gone?" In As-
pects of the Irish Theatre, eds. Patrick Rafroidi,
Raymonde Popot and William Parker. Lille: L'Université de Lille, 1972. P. 268.
Friel is seen as a successor to O'Casey and
other dramatists of the Irish Renaissance in his
ability to give Irish themes universal appeal.

_____, Bonnie K. Scott and Gordon Henderson. "The
Modern Drama." In Anglo-Irish Literature: A Review
of Research, ed. Richard J. Finneran. New York:
Modern Language Association, 1976. P. 552.
Friel is described as one of Ireland's most
popular living dramatists with a growing international reputation. Brief biographical and bibliographical facts are also provided.

Johnston, Denis. "Brian Friel and Modern Irish Drama."
Hibernia, 39 (n.d.), 5.
The famous elder statesman of Irish playwrit-
ing takes note of Friel's dramatic achievements.

Kai, Mariko. "The New Irish Plays: Brian Friel and John
B. Keane." Eibungaku, No. 37 (March 1972), 71-82.
Friel and Keane are discussed as emerging tal-
ents who draw imaginatively on Irish traditions
and everyday experience to create powerful drama.

Kenny, Herbert A. Literary Dublin: A History. Dublin:
Gill and MacMillan, 1974. Pp. 254, 281 and 282.
Kenny comments on the popularity of Philadel-
phia, Here I Come! and suggests The Loves of Cass
McGuire, though beautifully performed by actress
Ruth Gordon, was "too Irish in its essence for
American audiences."

Kerr, W. "One Plus One Equals One--about Philadelphia,
Here I come!" In Thirty Plays Hath November. New
York: Simon and Schuster, 1969. Pp. 113-17.
Kerr uses Philadelphia, Here I Come! as an
example of an unpretentious play that is neverthe-

less very affecting and he applauds Friel's clear
writing style and his warmhearted compassion.

Küsgen, Reinhardt. "Brian Friel: Philadelphia, Here I
Come!" In Das Englische Drama der Gegenwart: Interpretations. Ed. Horst Oppel. Berlin: Schmidt,
1976.
Küsgen says that Friel is one of the few new
Irish playwrights whose work is successful in other
countries. He notes the universal appeal of the
play of initiation into manhood.

Levin, Milton. "Brian Friel: an Introduction." Eire-
Ireland, 7 (Summer 1972), 132-36.
Levin provides a compact informative survey
of Friel's work, dramatic and non-dramatic, and
calls him modern Ireland's most important living
playwright. In commenting on Crystal and Fox,
which he calls a realistic tragedy, and The Mundy
Scheme, which is a "savage satire," Levin says
Friel is moving toward a dark and tragic view of
life.

McMahon, Sean. "The Black North." Eire-Ireland, 1
(Summer 1966), 63-74.
McMahon includes a brief survey of Friel's
work in his study of Northern Irish writers. He
notes useful biographical information but seems to
prefer Friel's short stories to his plays, believ-
ing Friel would be a worthy successor to Frank
O'Connor in that genre.

_____. "The New Irish Writers." Eire-Ireland, 9
(Spring 1974), 136-43.
Brian Friel's Freedom of the City is considered
a major Irish work of the past five years and Kilroy's The Big Chapel is described as a major modern
novel which draws convincingly on Irish history.

_____. "The Priest in Recent Irish Fiction." Eire-
Ireland, 3 (Summer 1968), 105-14.
Irish writers are attempting to depict the
changing role of the priest. Brian Friel's portrait
of the Canon in Philadelphia, Here I Come! as an
irrelevant outsider, and Edna O'Brien's various
priests and nuns are alluded to in the discussion.

Maxwell, D. E. S. Brian Friel. Lewisburg, Pa.: Bucknell University Press, 1975.
Maxwell provides a clear survey of Friel's
achievement to date, offering valuable biographical
and bibliographical information. Friel's basic
themes, both Irish and universal, are analyzed. He
is seen not as a political writer but as a sensitive

observer of life aware of man's struggle against
predetermined social obstacles.

_____. "Imagining the North. Violence and the
Writers." Eire-Ireland, 8 (Summer 1973), 91-107.
        Friel's works have political overtones: Ireland
is frigid--religiously and sexually. It is puritanical, joyless. Philadelphia, Here I Come!, The
Gentle Island, and A Saucer of Larks are all discussed in these terms, though Maxwell points out
that Friel's primary function is to present Ireland
spiritually and materially at a given time in history.

_____. "Introduction to The Enemy Within." Journal
of Irish Literature, 4 (May 1975), 4-6.
        Maxwell sees a movement in Friel toward a
greater involvement in contemporary Ireland's
political problems, but feels his grim subject matter in The Enemy Within is mitigated by the author's
humanity.

O'Malley, Mary. "Irish Theatre Letter." Massachusetts
Review, 6 (1964-65), 181-86.
        This is a history of the Abbey Theatre by its
"Artistic Director." Among recent productions have
been Brian Friel's The Enemy Within and Keane's
Many Young Men of Twenty. Both are praised as
works of promising native dramatists bringing new
life for the Abbey.

Ormsby, Frank. "The Plays of Brian Friel." Honest
Ulsterman, no. 23 (1974), 27-31.
        This is a survey of Friel's achievement in the
theatre, and his plea to encourage personal liber-
ties while preserving Irish traditions.

Warner, Alan. "Introducing Brian Friel." Acorn, no. 14
(November 1970), 25-28.
        Warner praises Friel as a fresh talent from
Northern Ireland.

II. REVIEWS

LOVERS

Billington, Michael. "A Tidy Pair." The Times,
26 August 1969, p. 10.
        Billington finds Losers (part II of
Lovers) "infinitely the better of the two
plays." A story of a subdued husband, who
taunts his oppressive mother-in-law by reveal-

ing that the Vatican no longer approves of her
favorite saint, succeeds because Friel "relates
an archetypal farcical episode to specific
Irish experience." Winners, which deals with
a boy and his pregnant girlfriend, who are
planning their marriage, is made maudlin by a
narrator who keeps interrupting with the news
that they will drown later on the same day.
Billington objects to a "folksiness" he finds
reminiscent of Wilder's Our Town.

Sullivan, Dan. "The Theatre: Art Carney and Lovers."
New York Times, 26 July 1968, p. 21.
Sullivan finds Friel's pair of one-act
plays entertaining, but slight. He objects to
the resemblance of Winners to certain aspects
of Our Town and he feels the basic situation
of Lovers is stereotyped.

THE LOVES OF CASS McGUIRE

Kerr, Walter. "The Theatre: Brian Friel's 'The
Loves of Cass McGuire.'" New York Times, 7
October 1966, p. 36.
Kerr's impression of the play is generally
favorable. He particularly relishes the irony
of a scene in which Cass discovers that the
most generous act of her lifetime, her weekly
contribution to her relatives, was never needed
and has been kept intact for her own use. The
depiction of the atmosphere of the rest home in
which Cass is eventually placed is convincing.

Wardle, Irving. "Brian Friel Returns to the Irish
American Dream." The Times, 13 October 1967,
p. 7.
Wardle calls Cass a companion piece to
Philadelphia, Here I Come! because both deal
with emigration and aspects of the "Irish
American dream." Cass McGuire worked as a
waitress for fifty years in America but always
sent home ten dollars a week out of her meager
wages. She returns home to find all of her old
friends genteel and affluent. Wardle notes:
"In America she has remained an Irish peasant;
in Ireland they have become Americanized."
Wardle regrets that the irony of the play is
dulled by Friel's sentimental portrait of Cass.
Ultimately he calls the play an attempt to
"translate a pathetic delusion into a noble
dream."

51

THE MUNDY SCHEME

Barnes, Clive. "The Mundy Scheme." New York Times, 12 December 1969, p. 75.

Calling "The Mundy Scheme" a "spectacle of scenes in search of a play," Barnes finds it shallow and "amateurish." It deals with an absurd plan by the Irish government to bury all the corpses of the world in the bogs of western Ireland. The joke is only momentarily funny and the portrayal of Irish political corruption is too trivial and unconvincing to be ironic. He concludes by calling Friel "Ireland's most talented young playwright" but insists the play itself was "sloppily conceived and constructed."

PHILADELPHIA, HERE I COME!

Hogan, Robert. "Philadelphia, Here I Come!" Eire-Ireland, 2 (Spring 1967), 92.

Hogan believes Friel has successfully integrated two Irish themes--"exile and the silence between generations" in an amusing and touching play. Like other critics he comments on Friel's use of Gar's "public" and "private" selves.

Kauffmann, Stanley. "'Philadelphia, Here I Come!' Arrives." New York Times, 17 February 1966, p. 28.

Friel has written a highly creditable play about a young Irishman bored with the empty rituals of Irish life, disappointed in love and alienated from his father. Kauffmann claims Friel offers no new insights into his emigration theme, only "novelty and not so novel at that." He praises only one scene--where Gar and his father, unable to sleep on the night prior to the boy's departure to the States, vainly make one last attempt to communicate. On the whole Kauffmann finds the play, like Friel's hero: "amiable and appealing enough but unexciting."

Kerr, Walter. "Philadelphia, Here I Come!" New York Herald Tribune, 17 February 1966, p. 10.

Kerr loves the play, especially the device of the alter-ego and the dialect speech: "the play is without pretense and it never cheats, doing exactly what it means to do very simply and very well."

Kilkenny Magazine, no. 14 (Spring-Summer 1966), 148-51.
     This review contains a lengthy plot sum-
mary and generally praises Friel and the actors
involved in this particular production.

John B. Keane

Born Listowel, July 21, 1928, Co. Kerry.

Inside Ireland Keane is, perhaps, the best known living Irish playwright. Audiences are charmed by his portraits of rural life and recognizable folk characters. A pub-owner, Keane combines a profitable business with a prolific output of plays, stories, and essays. His themes have an immediate bearing on everyday experiences. The subjects of emigration, arranged marriages, the breakdown of the family, and the exploitation of the weak are constantly explored, each time with fresh insight. He never moralizes but a sometimes bitter irony makes the author's stand a clear one. For Keane love and a sense of humor are the enduring constants in a productive life.

PRIMARY SOURCES

I. STAGE

"Backwater." Staged Cork, 1973.

_____. In Values. Cork: Mercier Press, 1973.

Big Maggie. Staged Cork, 1969; Los Angeles, 1976.

_____. Cork: Mercier Press, 1969.

The Change in Mame Fadden. Staged Cork and Chicago, 1971.

_____. Cork: Mercier Press, 1973.

The Crazy Wall. Staged Waterford, 1973.

_____. Dublin and Cork: Mercier Press, 1974.

Faoisemh. Dublin: Avel-Linn, n.d. (play in Irish).

The Field. Staged Dublin, 1965; New York, 1976.

_____. Cork: Mercier Press, 1966 and 1976.

The Good Thing. Staged Limerick, 1976.

_____. Cork: Mercier Press, 1976.

The Highest House on the Mountain. Staged Dublin, 1961.

_____. Dublin: Progress House, 1961.

Hut 42. Staged Dublin, 1963.

_____. Dixon, Ca.: Proscenium Press, 1963.

The Man from Clare. Staged Cork, 1963.

_____. Mercier Press, 1963.

Many Young Men of Twenty. Staged Cork, 1961.

_____. Dublin: Progress House, 1961.

_____. In Seven Irish Plays 1946-1964. Ed. Robert
   Hogan. Minneapolis: University of Minnesota
   Press, 1967.

Matchmaker. Staged Dublin, 1975.

Moll. Staged Killarney, County Kerry, 1971.

_____. Cork: Mercier Press, 1971.

No More in Dust. Staged Dublin, 1962.

The One-Way Ticket. Staged Listowel, County Kerry,
   1972.

"The Pure of Heart." Staged Cork, 1973.

_____. In Values. Cork: Mercier Press, 1973.

_____. In The Irish Press, 21 April 1975, n.p.

The Rain at the End of the Summer. Staged Cork, 1967.

_____. Cork: Mercier Press, 1967.

The Roses of Tralee. Staged Cork, 1966.

Sharon's Grave. Staged Cork, 1960; New York, 1962.

_____. Dublin: Progress House, 1960.

_____. In Seven Irish Plays 1946-1964. Ed. Robert
    Hogan. Minneapolis: University of Minnesota Press,
    1964.

Sive. Staged Listowel, County Kerry, 1959; London, 1961.

_____. Dublin: Progress House, 1959.

_____. Elgin, Illinois: Performance, n.d.

"The Springing of John O'Dorey." Staged Cork, 1973.

_____. In Values. Cork: Mercier Press, 1973.

Values: The Springing of John O'Dorey, Backwater,
    and The Pure of Heart. Staged Cork, 1973.

_____. Cork: Mercier Press, 1973.

The Year of the Hiker. Staged Cork and Chicago, 1964.

_____. Cork: Mercier Press, 1964.

II. RADIO

The Field, 2 March 1970, B.B.C. 4.

The War Crime, 9 January 1976, B.B.C. 4.

The Year of the Hiker, 11 January 1971, B.B.C. 4.

III. STORIES AND ESSAYS

"The Change." Journal of Irish Literature, 1 (May 1972),
    95-101.

"The Fort Field." Irish Press, 3 November 1975, n.p.

Death Be Not Proud and Other Stories. Dublin and Cork:
    Mercier Press, 1976.

The Gentle Art of Matchmaking and Other Important Things.
    Cork and Dublin: Mercier Press, 1973.

Is the Holy Ghost Really a Kerryman?   Cork: Mercier
    Press, 1973.

Letters of an Irish Civic Guard. Dublin and Cork:
    Mercier Press, 1976.

Letters of an Irish Parish Priest. Cork: Mercier Press,
    1972.

Letters of an Irish Publican. Dublin and Cork: Mercier
    Press, 1974.

Letters of a Love-Hungry Farmer. Dublin and Cork:
    Mercier Press, 1974.

Letters of a Matchmaker. Dublin and Cork: Mercier
    Press, 1975.

Letters of a Successful T. D. Cork: Mercier Press,
    1967.

Self-Portrait. Cork: Mercier Press, 1964, 1968.

Strong Tea. Cork: Mercier Press, 1963.

IV. POETRY

"Cat-Calls." Everyman, no. 1 (1968), 23-24.

"A Madman" and "Trapped Ones." Two Poems. Kilkenny
    Magazine, no. 3 (Spring 1961), 27-28.

The Street and Other Poems. Dublin: Progress Publica-
    tions, 1961.

SECONDARY SOURCES

I. CRITICISM

Brady, Seamus. "Are They Our Great Writers of Tomorrow?"
    Irish Digest, 79 (November 1963), 9-12.
        Keane is included (along with Friel) with three
    other modern successors to the writers of the Irish
    Renaissance (John McGahern, Richard Murphy, and

John O'Donovan) as battlers against the materialism
of the present time.

Cahill, Susan and Thomas Cahill. A Literary Guide to
Ireland. New York: Scribner's, 1973. P. 89.
    Reference is made to Keane's pub in Listowel,
a town where many Irish artists have lived, and
his plays Sive and Big Maggie are noted.

Colum, Padraic. "Theatre: Dublin." Theatre Arts, 44
(February 1960), 24-25.
    In this rambling article, Colum discusses two
plays: Maurice Mellon's Aisling and John B. Keane's
Sive. He gives a synopsis of each, singling out for
praise the characters of the matchmaker and the two
tinkers in Sive.

Coxe, Louis. "Letters from Dublin." The Nation, 26
March 1960, pp. 281-82.
    Coxe discusses the shortage of good plays in
Ireland. He makes brief mention of John B. Keane's
Sive, which--he says--"I delight in . . . if only
for the talk."

Encyclopedia of Ireland. Dublin: Allen Figgis, 1968.
    P. 378.
    Brief mention is made of Keane's contribution
to a native Irish drama.

Fallis, Richard. The Irish Renaissance. Syracuse:
Syracuse University Press, 1977. Pp. 181, 267, 271.
    Fallis comments on Keane's connection with the
Gate Theatre and the Southern Theatre Group in Cork.
He claims that Keane's work is characteristic of
mainstream Irish drama over the years, an honest
treatment of ordinary Irish experience. But he suggests Keane's work is too provincial to appeal to
non-Irish playgoers.

Fallon, Gabriel. "Dublin's Fourth Theatre Festival."
Modern Drama, 5 (May 1962), 21-26.
    Fallon calls Keane's No More in Dust "a compe-
tent piece of dramaturgy concerning the love life
of country girls in Dublin lodgings. . . ."

Fox, R. M. "Social Criticism in the Irish Theatre."
Aryan Path, 37 (December 1966), 179-81.
    Though Yeats banned plays of social criticism
from the Abbey in favor of drama emphasizing poetry
and rhetoric and while O'Casey carried on this tradition, J. B. Keane has begun a movement back to
social criticism in Irish drama.

Henderson, Joanne L. "Checklist of Four Kerry Writers: George Fitzmaurice, Maurice Walsh, Bryan MacMahon, and John B. Keane." Journal of Irish Literature, 1 (May 1972), 118-19 (Keane section). Brief but useful checklist which largely records primary sources.

Hogan, Robert. "The Hidden Ireland of John B. Keane." In After the Irish Renaissance: A Critical History of the Irish Drama Since The Plough and the Stars. Minneapolis: University of Minnesota Press, 1967. Pp. 208-20. Also in Eire-Ireland, 3 (Summer 1968), 14-26.
Hogan discusses Keane's enormous popularity in Ireland and summarizes his career. The pub-owner dramatist depicts greed with "cold accuracy" although he tends to be melodramatic at times. Hogan divides Keane's plays into three groups. The first group are plays like Sive which are influenced by Michael Molloy's naturalism. The second group like Hut 42 are realistic representations of modern life. The third group is composed of high-spirited musicals like Many Young Men of Twenty.

_____. "Where Have All the Shamrocks Gone?" In Aspects of the Irish Theatre. Eds. Patrick Rafroïdi, Raymonde Popot and William Parker. Lille: L'Université de Lille, 1972. Pp. 266-67.
Hogan discusses the influence of Irish playwright Molloy on Keane's work. Keane's career is a microcosm of the development of Irish drama in that his first plays attempted to recapture the past, his next ones showed the past losing out to the present, and finally in Mame Fadden his work moved into more universal areas.

_____, Bonnie K. Scott and Gordon Henderson. "The Modern Drama." In Anglo-Irish Literature: A Review of Research. Ed. Richard J. Finneran. New York: Modern Language Association, 1976. Pp. 551-52.
This provides a brief summary of Keane's works to date.

Kenny, Herbert A. Literary Dublin: A History. Dublin: Gill and MacMillan, 1974.
Keane is seen as a village playwright who nevertheless deals with universal themes.

Kinsman, Clare D. and Mary Ann Tennenhouse, eds. Contemporary Authors: A Bio-Bibliographical Guide to Current Authors and Their Works. Detroit: Gale

Research, 1972. Pp. 318-19.
  Keane is called Ireland's leading folk dramatist and a survey of his work is provided.

Linehan, Fergus. "Four Irish Playwrights." Irish
  Digest, 74 (April 1962), 84-87.
  Keane is the most popular playwright in Ire-
  land, though Behan is more popular abroad.

McGuiness, Arthur. "John Brendan Keane." In Contemporary Drama. Ed. James Vinson. London: St. James
  Press, 1977. Pp. 440-43.
  McGuiness provides a fine summary of Keane's
  achievement. He lists bibliographical material and
  provides helpful biography. Noting Keane's tremen-
  dous popularity in Ireland, McGuiness finds that in
  all his plays Keane is concerned with "the intimida-
  tion and exploitation of the weak by the strong" and
  points to the increasing darkness and irony of his
  vision.

Mercier, Vivian. "Foreword" to Aspects of the Irish
  Theatre. Eds. Patrick Rafroidi, Raymonde Popot and
  William Parker. Lille: L'Université de Lille,
  1972. P. 13.
  Mercier briefly alludes to Radio Éireann and
  its contribution to Keane's popularity.

O'Malley, Mary. See Friel bibliography above.

Pannecouche, Jean-Michel. "John Brendan Keane and the
  New Irish Rural Drama." In Aspects of the Irish
  Theatre. Eds. Patrick Rafroidi, Raymonde Popot and
  William Parker. Lille: L'Université de Lille,
  1972. Pp. 137-50.
  Keane's youth in County Kerry, his brief and
  unhappy emigration to England, and his work as a
  pub-keeper are all discussed in this article. From
  his play Sive, which was accepted for Radio Éireann,
  to the comic Big Maggie, Keane appears to be an
  ethnic writer who appeals primarily to Irish audiences. His thematic concerns--forced marriages,
  greed, social inequality, sexual frustration--are
  all related to "Ireland, Irish life, Irish society."

Rafroidi, Patrick. "Plays for Ireland." In Aspects of
  the Irish Theatre. Eds. Patrick Rafroidi, Raymonde
  Popot and William Parker. Lille: L'Université de
  Lille, 1972. Pp. 67-73.
  Rafroidi discusses the traditional connection
  between the theatre and nationalism in Ireland. He
  notes that Behan's The Hostage and Keane's Many
  Young Men of Twenty urged that Ireland should not
  remain so narrowly nationalistic and sectarian.

II. REVIEWS

BIG MAGGIE

    Drake, Sylvie. "Mother Alienates Brood in 'Maggie.'"
        Los Angeles Times, 18 May 1976, p. 8.
            "The production . . . is poorly realized
    and seems to have been hastily mounted and re-
    hearsed. . . . One wonders if it was worth it
    in the first place. Keane's play is a negative
    drama." Drake finds no psychological explora-
    tion to shed light on Maggie's behavior, "only
    perfunctory insights into the personalities of
    her grown children. . . . This play is a baf-
    fling and curiously unappealing piece of the-
    ater that is not enhanced by the Tara Players
    production."

THE HIGHEST HOUSE ON THE MOUNTAIN

    The Times, 24 September 1960, p. 10.
            Keane's characters always have the same
    primitive dignity one associates with the farm
    people in Millet's paintings. Keane cannot
    concentrate on a single theme, but this tale
    of hatred between brothers motivated by lust
    and greed has moments of power.

NO MORE IN DUST

    The Times, 21 September 1961, p. 16.
            There is brief mention of this play as
    marking the playwright's transfer of his lo-
    cale from Synge country to Dublin's left bank.
    The reviewer states that "appreciators of
    Keane's vitality welcome his break from paro-
    chialism."

THE RAIN AT THE END OF THE SUMMER

    The Times, 24 June 1967, p. 7.
            Keane changes his milieu in this play
    from rural Ireland to an urban setting where
    he concentrates on a Cork merchant-family fac-
    ing a social class dilemma and a father-son
    complication. After ten plays and two musicals
    Keane has written his first "social" play.
    The reviewer considers it less successful than
    his best rural dramas but a "starting point"
    in the playwright's development of new thematic
    material.

SHARON'S GRAVE

The Times, 22 April 1960, p. 18.
Keane's new play opening in Dublin does
not have the quality of Sive and the reviewer
laments, "Mr. Keane seems to have become 'gim-
mick' conscious." He adds that "the ingre-
dients of Sharon's Grave correspond rather too
closely to those which helped to make Sive
phenomenally successful with Irish audiences."
Although a feeling for the obviously grotesque
predominates over the complexity of character
creation, Keane shows "a sure instinct for
dramatic situations" and the last act is "grip-
ping in spite of the faults of the play."

Taubman, Howard. "'Sharon's Grave' Opens at the
Maidman." New York Times, 9 November 1961,
p. 39.
A play about grotesques, this "predictable
melodrama" fails to achieve the shocking dé-
nouement intended, yet it boasts two comic
characters, the crippled hunchback, Dinzie
Conlee, and the charlatan, Pats Bo Bwee, "who
creates a mood of grisly humor." Taubman notes
that the County Kerry pub keeper-dramatist has
"a vivid gift of Irish gab" and a "picturesque
flair" in his dialogue as he depicts the characters at a wake, a "digression into necro-
philia."

SIVE

New York Times, 6 September 1959, p. 11.
In Sive, his first successful play and
first play to reach the stage after a dozen
attempts, John B. Keane has caused as much ex-
citement and controversy as the early Sean
O'Casey. Although rejected by the Abbey,
Sive has met resounding praise as a full length
drama of a matchmaker who literally tries to
sell a young girl to an old farmer, accompanied
by a Greek chorus of two old tinkers. The rest
of the long review contains a preview of an am-
bitious second International Theater Festival
in Dublin after a hectic 1958 season.

Thomas Kilroy

Born September 23, 1934, Callan, Co. Kilkenny

    A distinguished teacher, scholar, and novelist,
Thomas Kilroy is moving toward the peak of his career.
Ten years ago The Death and the Resurrection of Mr.
Roche startled Irish audiences with its controversial
subject matter. His most recent play, Talbot's Box, a
stunning psychological study of a famous Irish martyr,
attests to his intrepid originality. He consciously
separates himself from the well-established naturalistic
school of Abbey playwrights. Many of his effects seem
to derive from expressionism, but he is eclectic and
constantly strives for new and unexpected sources of
drama. Nevertheless, his themes and characterizations
are intrinsically Irish. The traditions of his country
are sacred to him, and his mission appears to be to raise
the artistic and moral consciousness of his compatriots--
in the theatre, classroom, community, or wherever his
growing influence extends.

PRIMARY SOURCES

I. STAGE

The Death and Resurrection of Mr. Roche. Staged Dublin,
    1968. London: Faber and Faber, 1968.

_____. New York: Grove Press, 1968.

The O'Neill. Staged Dublin, 1969.

Talbot's Box. Staged Dublin, 1977.

Tea and Sex and Shakespeare. Staged Dublin, 1976.

II. RADIO

The Door. BBC Prizewinning radio play, 27 October 1967,
    Radio 4.

III. FICTION

The Big Chapel. London: Faber and Faber, 1971.

_____. London: Pan Books, 1971.

"Young Magdalen and the Pharisee." Threshold, No. 17,
    62-74.

IV. NONFICTION

"Fiction: 1967." University Review, 5 (Spring 1968),112-17.

"Groundwork for an Irish Theatre." Studies: An Irish
    Quarterly, 48 (Summer 1959), 192-98.

"Mervyn Wall: The Demands of Satire." Studies: An Irish
    Quarterly, 47 (Spring 1958), 83-89.

"Reading and Teaching the Novel." Studies: An Irish
    Quarterly, 56 (Winter 1967), 356-67.

Sean O'Casey: A Collection of Critical Essays. Ed., with
    an introduction by Thomas Kilroy. Twentieth Century
    Views Series. Teaneck, N.J.: Prentice-Hall, 1975.

"Synge and Modernism." J. M. Synge Centenary Papers,
    1971. Ed. Maurice Harmon. Dublin: Dolmen Press,
    1972. Pp. 167-79.

"Synge the Dramatist." Mosaic, v (1972), 9-16. Reprint-
    ed in From an Ancient to a Modern Theatre. Ed.
    R. G. Collins. Manitoba: University of Manitoba
    Press, 1972.

"Tellers of Tales." The Times Literary Supplement, 17
    March 1972, pp. 301-02.

"Two Playwrights: Yeats and Beckett." Myth and Reality
    in Irish Literature. Ed. Joseph Ronsley. Toronto:
    Wilfrid Laurier University Press, 1977. Pp. 183-95.

V. SELECTED REVIEWS BY KILROY

"Review of Plays of the Year, chosen by J. C. Trewin,
    and of The Hostage by Brendan Behan." Studies: An
    Irish Quarterly, 48 (Spring 1959), 111-13.

"Review of Reilly, poems by Desmond O'Grady." Studies:
    An Irish Quarterly, 51 (Spring 1962), 184-86.

"Review of W. B. Yeats and the Theatre of Desolate Real-
    ity by D. R. Clark and In Defense of Lady Gregory
    by Ann Saddlemeyer." Studies: An Irish Quarterly,
    55 (Winter 1966), 441-43.

"Review of Like Any Other Man by Patrick Boyle." Uni-
    versity Review, 4 (Spring 1967), 91-92.

"Review of Sean O'Faolain: A Critical Introduction, by
    Maurice Harmon." Dublin Magazine, 7 (Autumn-Winter
    1968), 98-100.

SECONDARY SOURCES

I. CRITICISM

Fallis, Richard. The Irish Renaissance. Syracuse:
    Syracuse University Press, 1977. P. 278.
        Fallis is primarily interested in Kilroy's
    novel, The Big Chapel, but points out Kilroy's ef-
    fective analysis of religious intolerance as a re-
    current literary theme and praises the author's
    insights into human psychology.

Fallon, Gabriel. "All This and the Abbey Too." Studies:
    An Irish Quarterly, 48 (Winter 1959), 434-42.
        Kilroy's arguments in his essay "Groundwork
    for the Irish Theatre" that the Irish theatre is
    not creative or noted in the society which supports
    it and is generally attuned to the mediocre are dis-
    puted here. Fallon defensively attacks all of Kil-
    roy's premises although he does not list any strong
    contemporary Irish plays or playwrights.

Harmon, Maurice. "By Memory Inspired: Themes and Forces
    in Recent Irish Writing." Eire-Ireland, 8 (Summer
    1973), 3-19.
        Kilroy is one of a number of Irish writers who
    draw on traditional Irish themes.

Hogan, Robert. "Where Have All the Shamrocks Gone?" In
Aspects of the Irish Theatre. Eds. Patrick Rafroidi, Raymonde Popot and William Parker. Lille:
L'Université de Lille, 1972. P. 269.
Hogan briefly mentions The Death and Resurrection of Mr. Roche and Kilroy's second play, an
historical melodrama, about the great O'Neill.

_____, Bonnie K. Scott and Gordon Henderson. "The
Modern Drama." In Anglo-Irish Literature: A Review
of Research. Ed. Richard J. Finneran. New York:
Modern Language Association, 1976. P. 552.
Kilroy is briefly noted as an artist who is
both a prize-winning novelist and a playwright.
The Death and Resurrection of Mr. Roche is described
as his "most notable" play.

Maxwell, D. E. S. See John Boyd bibliography above.

_____. Brian Friel. Lewisburg: Bucknell University
Press, 1973. Pp. 107-08.
Maxwell believes a more relaxed attitude in
Irish society, particularly concerning sex, has
enabled playwrights like Kilroy to explore formerly
taboo subjects, such as homosexuality in The Death
and Resurrection of Mr. Roche.

II. REVIEWS

THE DEATH AND RESURRECTION OF MR. ROCHE

Wardle, Irving. "Irish Residents and Exiles." The
Times, 12 October 1968, p. 23.
Resident playwrights' subjects may be
repetitive, but they speak for community and
sometimes hit on "an urgent and unexploited
theme," as Kilroy has done in Death and Resurrection of Mr. Roche. Wardle comments, "its
subject is that all-too-familiar and depressing
Irish custom of the all-male drinking fraternity, yet this seems to be the first time that
it has been directly treated on the Irish
stage." Wardle adds, "The play is not about
latent homosexuality but about a general flight
from life. . . . I suppose it will be considered too Irish for export . . . bristles with
local gags . . . dialogue is largely composed
of breezy clichés put together to reflect the
desolation and shyness underlying the mask of
virility." On the other hand, he finds it no
more local than Chayefsky's The Bachelor

<u>Party</u>. In summary, it is "one of the few im-
portant new plays the festival has launched."

TALBOT'S BOX

Chaillet, Ned. "Dublin Festival Finds a Winner."
   <u>The Times</u>, 17 October 1977, p. 7.
         Chaillet very briefly discusses a written
   script since the reviewer left the festival
   before <u>Talbot's Box</u> had been performed, but
   he predicts it will be controversial and successful. "Sharp, pointed, and funny examina-
   tion of Matthew Talbot. . . . If Mr. Kilroy's
   somewhat over-written script plays as well as
   it reads it should keep the Abbey's small
   Peacock theatre filled."

TEA AND SEX AND SHAKESPEARE

<u>The Times</u>, 11 October 1976, p. 10.
         Here Kilroy "explores the barren terrain
   of a writer's block." A day and night in the
   life of a Dublin novelist is the play's subject matter; its jokes are laboriously constructed and it generally fails to please the
   reviewer.

Hugh Leonard

Born John Keyes Byrne November 9, 1926, Dublin, Co. Dublin.

Hugh Leonard's work may be more familiar to American and British audiences than that of any other Irish writer in this volume, although they might not be able to identify him by name. His television script-writing has been so prodigious that nearly all devotees of B.B.C. television drama or Masterpiece Theatre have spent pleasurable hours listening to his dialogue or generally appreciating both his adaptations and original productions. Dickens's Dombey and Son, Great Expectations, and Nicholas Nickleby, Wilkie Collins's The Moonstone, and Dostoevsky's The Possessed are among his better known contributions. He also wrote numerous series shows such as Me Mammy and Jezebel Ex-UK. No stranger to the legitimate stage, he has contributed consistently to the theatre in Dublin and London for the past two decades. His most recent popular success, Da, was staged first in Dublin and Washington, D.C., five years ago, but a handsome New York production has finally gained him the recognition he deserves from American audiences. His mastery of complicated stage devices, such as the use of multiple actors playing one character, is combined with a simple and direct message--the need for his contemporaries to cultivate self-knowledge, discipline, and tolerance, thereby preserving human contacts and feelings.

PRIMARY SOURCES

I. STAGE

All the Nice People. Staged Dublin, 1966, as Mick and
    Nick.

_____. In Plays and Players, 14 (December 1966).

The Au Pair Man. Staged Dublin, 1968; London, 1969; New
York, 1973.

_____. In Plays and Players, 43 (December 1968).

_____. In Plays and Players: Plays 1966-69. London:
Plays and Players, 1970.

_____. New York: Samuel French, 1974.

The Barracks. Staged Dublin, 1969.

The Big Birthday. Staged Dublin, 1956.

Da. Staged Dublin and Washington, D.C., 1973.

_____. In Plays and Players, 45 (December 1973).

_____. Newark, Delaware: Proscenium Press, 1976.

Dublin One [adaptation from Dubliners by Joyce]. Staged
Dublin, 1963.

The Family Way. Staged Dublin, 1964; London, 1966.

Irishmen: A Suburb of Babylon. A trilogy including
Irishmen, Nothing Personal, The Last of the Last of
the Mohicans. Staged Dublin, 1975.

The Italian Road. Staged Dublin, 1954.

The Late Arrival of the Incoming Aircraft (televised
1964). London: Evans, 1968.

A Leap in the Dark. Staged Dublin, 1957.

Liam Liar [adaptation of the play Billy Liar by Keith
Waterhouse and Willis Hall]. Staged Dublin, 1976.

Madigan's Lock. Staged Dublin, 1958; London, 1963.

Mick and Mick [sic]. In Plays and Players: Plays 1966-
69. London, 1970.

The Passion of Peter McGinty. Staged Dublin, 1961.

The Patrick Pearse Motel. Staged Dublin and London,
1971; Washington, D.C., 1972.

_____. In Plays and Players, 18 (May 1971).

_____. In Plays of the Year. Ed. J. C. Trewin. Vol.
41. London: Elek Books, 1972.

_____. London: Samuel French, 1972.

The Poker Session. Staged Dublin, 1963; London, 1964; New York, 1967.

_____. In Plays and Players, 2 (1964).

_____. London: Evans, 1963.

_____. London: Hansom Books, 1964.

_____. In Plays of the Year, 1963-64. Ed. J. C. Trewin. Vol. 28. London: Elek Books, 1965.

The Quick, and the Dead. Staged Dublin, 1967.

The Saints Go Cycling In [adaptation of the novel The Dalkey Archives by Flann O'Brien]. Staged Dublin, 1965.

Some of My Best Friends Are Husbands [adaptation of a play by Eugene Labiche]. Staged London, 1976.

Stephen D [adaptation of A Portrait of the Artist as a Young Man and Stephen Hero by James Joyce]. Staged Dublin, 1962; London, 1963; New York, 1967.

_____. London: Evans, 1962.

_____. In Two Ages of Man. Ed. A. W. England. London: Oliver, 1971.

"Stiphin Didalus." Al-Masrah, 71 (April 1970).

Summer. Staged Dublin, 1974.

A Walk on the Water. Staged Dublin, 1960.

II. TELEVISION PLAYS AND SERIES (Exact broadcast dates listed when available from B.B.C. archives.)

Another Fine Mess, 22 April 1973.

Assassin, 10 January 1968.

The Bitter Pill, 1973.

Blackmail series, 1965.

Conan Doyle series: The Hound of the Baskervilles, 30 September-7 October 1968.

The Corpse Can't Play, 3 May 1968.

Do You Play Requests?, 1964.

Dombey and Son (serialization), from the novel by Dickens, 17 August-19 November 1969.

The Ghost of Christmas Present, 1972.

Great Big Blond, 1965.

Great Expectations (serialization), from the novel by Dickens, 22 January-22 March 1967.

The Hammer of God, The Actor and the Alibi, The Eye of Apollo, The Forbidden Garden, The Three Tools of Death, and The Quick One (Father Brown series), 1974.

The Hidden Truth series, 1964.

The Higgler, 1973.

High Kampf, 28 August 1973.

Hunt the Peacock, with H. R. Keating, 12 October 1969.

I Loved You Last Summer, 1965.

The Informer series, 1966.

Insurrection (8 parts), 1966.

The Irish Boys (trilogy), 1962.

Jezebel Ex-UK series, 1963.

Judgement Day, 1973.

A Kind of Kingdom, 1963.

The Late Arrival of the Incoming Aircraft, 25 November 1965.

The Liars series, 1966.

The Lodger and The Judge (Simenon series), 19 June 1966 and 19 July 1966, respectively.

Love Life, 1967.

A Man and His Mother-in-Law, 31 May 1968.

Me Mammy, 14 June 1968.

Milo O'Shea, 1973.

The Moonstone (serialization), from the novel by Wilkie
      Collins, 16 January-13 February 1972.

My One True Love, 14 March 1964.

Nicholas Nickleby (serialization), from the novel by
      Dickens, 11 February-5 May 1968.

No Such Things as a Vampire, 19 April 1968.

Our Miss Fred, 1972.

Out of the Unknown series, 1966-67.

Pandora, 1971.

Percy, 1971.

The Possessed (serialization), from the novel by Dostoev-
      sky, 23 January-6 March 1969.

Public Eye, 1965.

Realm of Error, 1964.

The Removal Person, 1971.

The Retreat, 1966.

Saki series, 1962.

Second Childhood, 10 November 1966.

The Second Wall, 17 March 1964.

A Sentimental Education (serialization), from the novel
      by Flaubert, 14 August-4 September 1970.

Silent Song, 2 February 1966.

The Sinners series, 1970-71.

Somerset Maugham series: P & O, 1969 ; Jane, 30 April 1970.

Stone Cold Sober, 1973.

The Sullen Sisters, 1972.

Tales from the Lazy Acres series, 10 April-29 May 1972.

Talk of Angels, 1969.

A Time of Wolves and Tigers, 6 December 1967.

The Travelling Woman, 1973.

A Triple Irish, 10 June 1964.

The Trugh Game, 1972.

Undermind series, 1964.

The View from the Obelisk, 1964.

The Virgins, 1972.

The Watercress Girl, from the story by H. E. Bates, 1972.

White Walls and Olive Green Carpets, 1971.

Wuthering Heights (serialization), from the novel by Emily
      Bronte, 28 October-18 November 1967.

III.   FILM

Great Catherine, 1968.   Warner Brothers, A Jules Bach-
      Peter O'Toole Production.

Interlude, 1968.   Columbia Pictures, A David Deutsch Pro-
      duction.

IV.   INTERVIEW

Hickey, Des and Gus Smith.   A Paler Shade of Green.
      London: Leslie Frewin, 1972. Pp. 191-201.
         In this most informative interview, Leonard
      provides us with his family history and anecdotes
      of his early years, his employment in the Civil
      Service, the rejection of an early play by the
      Abbey. He describes the writing of Stephen D and
      his work on famous B.B.C. television serials, as
      well as his present and future writing plans.

SECONDARY SOURCES

I.   CRITICISM

Bennett, Robert B.   "Da." Journal of Irish Literature,
      5 (September 1976), 148-49.
         Bennett calls Da "a play of polished sensibil-

ity, inventiveness, and theatrical craftsmanship,"
and he discusses the paradox of cruelty in kindness
which underlies Da's relationship to his playwright
son.

Billington, Michael. "Hugh Leonard." In Contemporary
Drama. Ed. James Vinson. London: St. James Press,
1977. Pp. 478-82.
This essay includes a lengthy list of Leonard's
television credits and stage plays. Billington
provides a brief biography of Leonard and points
out his prolific contribution to the entertainment
industry within the British Isles.

Caswell, Robert W. "Unity and the Irish Theatre."
Studies: An Irish Quarterly, 49 (Spring 1960), 63-67.
Caswell tends to support playwright Kilroy's
negative view of the Irish theatre in 1960, but he
does single out Leonard's Madigan's Lock for special
praise because he believes it makes a fresh use of
"the best in his own [the Irish playwright's] tradition."

Encyclopedia of Ireland. Dublin: Allen Figgis, 1968.
P. 378.
This contains a brief reference to Leonard as
an important writer of stage and television plays.

Fallis, Richard. The Irish Renaissance. Syracuse:
Syracuse University Press, 1977. P. 273.
Fallis defends Leonard's extensive work in
television and calls him "a highly professional
theatre man." Stephen D is singled out for special
praise.

Fallon, Gabriel. See Keane bibliography above.

Fitzgerald, Marion. "Playwriting Is Agony Says Hugh
Leonard." Irish Digest, 79 (December 1963), 34-36.
Leonard acknowledges the satisfaction his success in the theatre and in television has brought
him, but complains of the fatigue and continual
need for self-discipline associated with a life in
the arts. His own favorite playwrights are Pinter,
Williams, and O'Casey in descending order.

Hewes, Henry. See Behan bibliography above.

Hickey, Des and Gus Smith. A Paler Shade of Green.
London: Leslie Frewin, 1972. Pp. 177-79.
This is essentially an interview with actor
Norman Rodway about his experience of playing

Stephen in Leonard's Stephen D. It provides some
insights into the popular reception of the play.

Hogan, Robert. After the Irish Renaissance: A Critical
    History of the Irish Drama Since The Plough and
    the Stars. Minneapolis: University of Minnesota
    Press, 1967. Pp. 186-89.
        Hogan provides a resumé of Leonard's prolific
    career as a playwright. He criticizes A Walk on
    the Water for being a "technical excuse" but
    praises Stephen D as "one of the most impressive
    plays to appear in Dublin since the war." Leonard
    is technically more proficient than his contempo-
    raries, Hogan argues, but sometimes falls into a
    "pat commercialism."

_____. "Dublin: The Summer Season and the Theatre
    Festival, 1967." See Friel bibliography above.

_____. "Where Have All the Shamrocks Gone?" In As-
    pects of the Irish Theatre. Eds. Patrick Rafroïdi,
    Raymonde Popot and William Parker. Lille: L'Uni-
    versité de Lille, 1972. Pp. 267-68, 270.
        Leonard is called "perhaps the most profession-
    al of the newer dramatists" in the sense that he
    has wide success outside of Ireland, especially
    writing television shows for the B.B.C. His the-
    matic eclecticism is considered "symptomatic of
    the Irish playwright's uncomfortable search for a
    subject."

_____, Bonnie K. Scott and Gordon Henderson. "The
    Modern Drama." Anglo-Irish Literature: A Review of
    Research. Ed. Richard J. Finneran. New York:
    Modern Language Association, 1976. P. 551.
        Leonard's popular success in writing scenes and
    shows for the B.B.C. is noted. His major dramatic
    works are praised for their variety, professional
    style, and widespread appeal.

Kenny, Herbert A. Literary Dublin: A History. Dublin:
    Gill and MacMillan, 1974. Pp. 282-83.
        Leonard's work is briefly characterized as
    having "high literary cachet" in Dublin.

Roberts, Peter. See Murphy bibliography below.

Rushe, Desmond. "Dublin Theatre Festival." Eire-Ireland,
    8 (Winter 1973), 146-48.
        Leonard's Da (along with Michael MacLiammoir's
    Prelude to Kazbek Street) was one of the two best
    plays presented during the September 1973 Dublin
    Theatre Festival.

II. REVIEWS

THE AU PAIR MAN

Kerr, Walter. New York Times, 13 January 1974,
p. 11.
Kerr calls The Au Pair Man a "play about
props." The characters are "handy coins to be
shuffled about by the author." Kerr objects to
the play's allegory in which the hero-bill-
collector is actually Ireland and the greedy
landlady represents England.

Wardle, Irving. "Dublin Satire on the Monarchy."
The Times, 8 October 1968, p. 6.
The Au Pair Man is a satire on the British
monarchy, which Dublin critics "mistook for a
straight light comedy." This does not surprise
Wardle because he feels the play's allegory in-
volves both England's assimilation of the
"angry" generation and England's trouble with
Ireland. The two levels of meaning "cancel
each other out."

THE BIG BIRTHDAY

The Times, 27 January 1956, p. 7.
The reviewer comments: "Mr. Leonard's
third act is by far his best, as it speeds to
an uproarious finish. . . . His particular
talent lies in characterization, which augurs
well for future work. He should do well as a
writer of serious plays, for which he has the
technique, the sense of timing, and the ability
to write dialogue. He rather wastes his tal-
ents, perhaps, on farcical comedy."

DA

Gussow, Mel. "'Da' Gets a New Life on Broadway."
New York Times, 2 May 1978, p. 46.
Da draws praise from Gussow, who, perhaps
hyperbolically, states that it is "in a class
with the best of Sean O'Casey." In this auto-
biographical comedy, full of many levels of
consciousness and abrupt changes in time, the
theme is the "varieties of familial love and
the tricks and distortions of memory." Barnard
Hughes, as "Da," gets particular acclaim for
his performance in a rare production which has
"not been artificially enlarged for Broadway."

T. E. Kalem, Time, 15 May 1978, p. 78.
    Kalem calls Da a "fencing match with the
ghosts of the past" emphasizing the play's
themes of the depth of familial and racial
attachment, memory, and the passage of time.
Kalem feels that Leonard is typically Irish in
that his sense of "loss is borne with a salty
wit and exuberantly wild fantasy," but, sig-
nificantly, states that he is a "lesser" dramatist than O'Casey. Special praise is reserved
for the cast.

IRISHMEN: A SUBURB OF BABYLON

    Peter, John. "Delightful Debut." The Sunday Times,
        12 October 1975, p. 37.
            Peter notes: "Mr. Leonard is back on his
    favorite ground, Dublin suburbia. With lo-
    quacious specimens of the Irish middle class
    torn between petty debauchery and nagging con-
    sciences." The second act he feels is a new
    departure for Leonard with its "chilling topi-
    cality." The third act returns to semi-farce.
    Yet we are left with the sense Leonard has
    seen "something terrifying."

A LEAP IN THE DARK

    The Times, 25 January 1957, p. 3.
            The reviewer calls this play "a political
    thriller" with a theme that is "extremely
    topical." He notes that it is unusual for an
    Abbey play to plunge directly into the world
    of current Irish political unrest.

MADIGAN'S LOCK

    The Times, 29 March 1958, p. 3.
            The reviewer praises Leonard's growing
    skills as a dramatist and his blending of
    realism with fantasy, which recalls a favorite
    technique of Denis Johnston. In this play the
    hero's phantom fiancée speaks "remarkably beau-
    tiful lines."

THE PASSION OF PETER McGINTY

    The Times, 21 September 1961, p. 16.
            The reviewer comments: "Mr. Leonard,
    having made due acknowledgment to Ibsen and

Peer Gynt, proceeds to a shameless and quite
funny plagiarization of such old Irish masters
as O'Casey and Denis Johnston, adding a side-
swipe or two at Tennessee Williams and Arthur
Miller, and throwing several hefty bricks at
sundry respected Irish institutions." He goes
on to note that the troll king's impersonation
of Brendan Behan is highly amusing and not in
poor taste.

THE PATRICK PEARSE MOTEL

Wardle, Irving. "'The Patrick Pearse Motel,' Play
about Ireland, Is Staged in London." New York
Times, 19 June 1971, p. 16.
Leonard has "repeatedly exploited the
comic collision between traditional and modern
Ireland, but never so thoroughly as in this
satiric farce on television and real estate."
The Mother Ireland Motels, complete with steak
dinners in the "Famine Room" and recalcitrant
plumbers who refuse to install bidets, become
the subject of a beautifully written, hilarious
comedy.

THE POKER SESSION

Young, B. A. "Hugh Leonard Play in London Premiere."
New York Times, 12 February 1964, p. 30.
Basically a comedy-thriller, The Poker
Session is a very black comedy and Leonard's
"foolery" sometimes intrudes on the serious
action. The play is well-written but not always entertaining. It deals with a mental
patient who mounts "a grotesque charade with
the object of unearthing the grim circumstances
beneath his family's suburban respectability
that led to his mental collapse."

The Times, 15 February 1969, p. 19.
This is a brief mention of a radio performance of the play. The reviewer feels it
is "entirely lacking in innocence (though not
perhaps in naivete), kindliness or indeed any
human feeling worth having."

STEPHEN D

Smith, Hugh. "Joyce's 'Stephen' Staged in Dublin."
New York Times, 25 September 1962, p. 31.
Leonard's play was well received at the

81

Gate. Norman Rodway's performance as Stephen
was praised and the play was described as a
series of two-hour vignettes drawn from materials in Stephen Hero and Portrait of the
Artist as a Young Man.

The Times, 13 February 1963, p. 13.
    The reviewer feels Leonard's play is the
most effective Joyce adaptation to date.
Joyce's book was a "spiritual autobiography"
and Leonard, sensing this, has placed action in
Stephen's mind. The playwright's timing and
sense of the dramatic line is "unfailing."

SUMMER

Lewsen, Charles. "Dublin Theatre Festival." The
    Times, 11 October 1974, p. 17.
    Lewsen much prefers this play to Edna
O'Brien's The Gathering, produced at the same
festival. Although he considers the plot
"contrived," he finds "real authority in
Leonard's last cynical moments."

James McKenna

Born June 1933, Dublin, Co. Dublin.

James McKenna has combined important careers as a
writer and sculptor. He was educated in Kilcoole and
Bray and was awarded a Macaulay Fellowship in Sculpture
from the College of Art in 1960. In the same year he
helped to found the Independent Artists and exhibits
with them; the Irish Times has called him "the best stone
sculptor in Ireland today." The Scatterin' won praise at
the 1960 Dublin Theatre Festival. Music and dancing
added to the exuberance of the first production, which is
an expressionistic treatment of the emigration scene.
McKenna called his second play, At Bantry, a "mask-play"
and he founded a mask-theatre group called Rising Ground.
At Bantry is written in free verse and in recent years
McKenna has written highly· acclaimed poetry. His work
attests to the variety and complexity of the new Irish
stage.

PRIMARY SOURCES

I. STAGE

At Bantry. Staged Dublin, 1967.

_____. Dublin: B. M. MacThormand, 1968.

The Battering Ram. Staged Dublin, 1977.

Citizen's Tree. Staged Dublin, 1972.

The Scatterin'. Staged Dublin, 1960; Stratford East,
        1962.

_____. Co. Kildare: Goldsmith Press, 1977.

83

II. RADIO

Hotep Comes from the River, 1969, Radio Eireann.

III. POETRY

Crisis: Poem, Drawing and Script. Dublin: Goldsmith
    Press, 1974.

Poems. With drawings by the author. Dublin: Goldsmith
    Press, 1973; reprinted 1975.

SECONDARY SOURCES

I. CRITICISM

Donoghue, Denis. "Dublin Letter." The Hudson Review,
    13 (Winter 1960-61), 579-85.
        The author discusses the state of Irish drama.
    He has praise for the actor Michael MacLiammóir and
    slurring comments for Behan. He is ambivalent about
    James McKenna, whose play The Scatterin' was a part
    of the Dublin International Theatre Festival;
    Donoghue writes: "Mr. McKenna's theme is the frus-
    tration of Dublin's young men in a country endowed
    with nothing but an incandescent past. . . . As a
    derivative piece the play had its moments. . . ."

Hewes, Henry. "Broadway Postscript." Saturday Review,
    10 September 1960, pp. 33, 36.
        Hewes makes a few remarks about Behan, Hugh
    Leonard, and James McKenna. McKenna's play The
    Scatterin'--"About some Dublin rock-'n'-rollers"--
    is opening at the Pike. Leonard is a "quietly angry
    young man," who writes soap-operas to finance his
    playwriting. And Behan is "faced with the daily
    task of living up to his reputation as a bad lad."

Hogan, Robert. After the Irish Renaissance: A Critical
    History of the Irish Drama Since The Plough and the
    Stars. Minneapolis: University of Minnesota Press,
    1967. Pp. 35, 182, 185, 197, 265n.
        McKenna is fleetingly described as a talented
    young dramatist, a product of the Dublin Theatre
    Festival, the creator of a Dublin-type "teddy boy."
    McKenna's almost expressionistic use of stage space
    is noted.

_____, Bonnie K. Scott and Gordon Henderson. "The Modern Drama." In Anglo-Irish Literature: A Review of Research. Ed. Richard J. Finneran. New York: Modern Language Association, 1976. P. 522.
    McKenna's work is briefly surveyed. He is referred to as a sculptor-playwright, very much a part of Dublin's artistic life.

Linehan, Fergus. "Four Irish Playwrights." Irish Digest, 74 (April 1962), 84-87.
    This article discusses Behan, Keane, and Donagh MacDonagh as well as McKenna. Linehan says that McKenna may be forging a new style in Irish drama.

II. REVIEWS

AT BANTRY

Hogan, Robert. "Dublin: The Summer Season and Theatre Festival, 1967." Drama Survey, 6 (Spring 1968), 315-23.
    Hogan finds At Bantry a disappointing play, faulting its "undistinguished free verse." He believes McKenna has not lived up to the promise of his first play, The Scatterin'.

THE SCATTERIN'

"Play on Irish Youth Landed in Dublin." New York Times Theater Reviews, 15 September 1960, p. 44.
    This is a brief note on the Dublin opening of this "musical-with-drama fantasy," which elicited praise from Irish critics. Seamus Kelly of The Irish Times called it the "most exciting play since The Plough and the Stars of O'Casey" and Patrick Glennon of The Irish Independent described it as a "sprawling, vital, vivid theatrical tour de force, part O'Casey, part intimate review, even part music hall." The story line, focused on Dublin youths who are forced to immigrate to Britain, is accompanied by rock 'n' roll music by Dublin composer Arthur J. Potter.

Hewes, Henry. Saturday Review, 15 October 1960, p. 35.
    In The Scatterin' Dublin's six Teddy boys are not so much angry as they are "lonely and directionless," Hewes claims. He finds the

interruptions of story and dialogue by rock 'n'
roll music appealing and he adds that "The
Story of Biddy the Whore" is a show-stopper.

Thomas Murphy

Born February 23, 1935, Tuam, Co. Galway.

Thomas Murphy grew up on a big housing estate in
Tuam and claims that an awareness of emigration was the
obsession of his youth. He left school to work in a
sugar factory when he was eighteen but eventually won
a scholarship to continue his education. He also taught
school for more than four years. One reason for his
leaving Ireland was a chance to do a television drama on
the Congo which never materialized. Nevertheless he
contributed radio and television plays to the B.B.C.
His first notable success on the legitimate stage was
A Whistle in the Dark, which opened in London in 1961 and
was later performed successfully in New York. It con-
tained a penetrating analysis of the roots of violence
in modern life. Much of his work has a chilling, suspenseful quality. He frequently satirizes priest-ridden
provincials and is equally critical of the demeaning
treatment of women in past and present societies. In
his play The White House he interjects the death of
President Kennedy into a play about life in an Irish
pub. He believes his separation from Ireland has allowed
him to evaluate his background objectively without
diminishing his affection for his native country.

PRIMARY SOURCES

I. STAGE

Famine. Staged Dublin, 1966; London, 1969.

The Fooleen: A Crucial Week in the Life of a Grocer's
 Assistant. Staged Dublin, 1969; California, 1971.

_____. Dixon, Ca.: Proscenium Press, 1970.

The Morning After Optimism. Staged Dublin, 1971; New York, 1974.

_____. Cork: Mercier Press, 1973.

On the Inside. Staged Dublin, 1974.

_____. In On the Outside/On the Inside. Dublin: Gallery Books, 1976.

On the Outside, with Noel O'Donoghue. Staged Cork, 1961; Dublin, 1974; New Haven, Conn., 1976.

_____. In On the Outside/On the Inside. Dublin: Gallery Books, 1976.

The Orphans. Staged Dublin, 1968; Newark, Delaware, 1971.

_____. Newark, Delaware: Proscenium Press, 1974.

_____. Journal of Irish Literature, 3 (September 1974).

The Sanctuary Lamp. Staged Dublin, 1975.

_____. Dublin: Poolbeg Press, 1976.

The Vicar of Wakefield [adaptation of the novel by Goldsmith]. Staged Dublin, 1974.

A Whistle in the Dark. Staged London, 1961; New York, 1969.

_____. New York: Samuel French, 1971.

The White House. Staged Dublin, 1972.

II. TELEVISION (Exact broadcast dates listed when available from B.B.C. archives.)

A Crucial Week in the Life of a Grocer's Assistant, 1967. 22 March 1967.

Conversations on a Homecoming, 1976.

The Fly Sham, 19 May 1963.

The Moral Force, The Policy, Relief (trilogy), 1973.

Snakes and Reptiles, 14 April 1968.

Speeches of Farewell, 1976.

<u>A</u> <u>Trilogy</u> (<u>The</u> <u>Moral</u> <u>Force</u>, <u>The</u> <u>Policy</u>, <u>Relief</u>), 1973.

<u>Veronica</u>, 3 November 1963.

<u>Young</u> <u>Man</u> <u>in</u> <u>Trouble</u>, 1970.

III. FILM

<u>The</u> <u>Sun-Eaters</u>, 1971.

<u>Wrack</u>, 1972.

IV. RADIO

<u>Famine</u>, 3 March 1971, B.B.C. Radio 4.

V. INTERVIEW

Hickey, Des and Gus Smith. <u>A</u> <u>Paler</u> <u>Shade</u> <u>of</u> <u>Green</u>.
     London: Leslie Frewin, 1972. Pp. 225-27.
          Murphy discusses his major themes of emigration
     and violence. He accounts for his leaving Dublin
     at an early age and the objectivity this has given
     him about his country. He discusses his isolated
     position as an Irishman living in England, the
     writing of <u>Whistle</u> <u>in</u> <u>the</u> <u>Dark</u> and <u>The</u> <u>Orphans</u>, and
     his struggles with a lingering provincialism.

SECONDARY SOURCES

I. CRITICISM

Armstrong, W. A. "The Irish Point of View: The Plays of
     Sean O'Casey, Brendan Behan and Thomas Murphy."
     <u>Experimental</u> <u>Drama</u>. London: Bell, 1963. Pp. 79-
     102.
          Murphy shares with O'Casey and Behan a preoccu-
     pation with defects in the Irish Establishment, such
     as censorship and prudery, dead traditions, and
     "violence by religious superstition and tribal codes
     of conduct." Murphy's <u>Whistle</u> <u>in</u> <u>the</u> <u>Dark</u> is dis-
     cussed in some detail.

Elsom, John. "Thomas Murphy." In Contemporary Dramatists. Ed. James Vinson. London: St. James Press,
1977. Pp. 583-86.
　　　Elsom believes Murphy is the best Irish dramatist since O'Casey but like O'Casey sometimes "moves
away from his surefooted skills toward a more tenta-
tive allegory." At his best Murphy is a naturalistic writer who combines a penetrating social awareness with a "carefully organized dramatic technique."

Fallis, Richard. The Irish Renaissance. Syracuse:
Syracuse University Press, 1977. P. 273.
　　　Murphy's Whistle in the Dark is noted as a
worthy exception to what Fallis considers the de-
clining "health" of the Irish theatre.

Hogan, Robert. "Where Have All the Shamrocks Gone?" In
Aspects of the Irish Theatre. Eds. Patrick Rafroidi,
Raymonde Popot and William Parker. Lille: L'Université de Lille, 1972. P. 265.
　　　Hogan praises Murphy as a leading young dramatist, especially for his sensitive treatment of the
emigration theme.

_____, Bonnie K. Scott and Gordon Henderson. "The
Modern Drama." In Anglo-Irish Literature: A Review
of Research. Ed. Richard J. Finneran. New York:
Modern Language Association, 1976. P. 552.
　　　Murphy's major works are listed.

Kenny, Herbert A. Literary Dublin: A History. Dublin:
Gill and MacMillan, 1974. P. 282.
　　　In a brief mention Whistle in the Dark is
called Murphy's major play.

Mercier, Vivian. "Foreword" to Aspects of the Irish
Theatre. Eds. Patrick Rafroidi, Raymonde Popot and
William Parker. Lille: L'Université de Lille,
1972. P. 14.
　　　Mercier applauds the contemporary relevance
of A Whistle in the Dark and comments on Murphy's
naturalistic language.

Roberts, Peter. "Dublin 2." Plays and Players, 18 (May
1971), 53-55.
　　　Roberts discusses the 13th annual Dublin
Theatre Festival. Thomas Murphy's The Morning After
Optimism is among the plays presented--as is Hugh
Leonard's The Patrick Pearse Motel. Roberts likes
both.

Welch, Robert. "On the Outside/On the Inside." *Irish*
University Review, 7 (Spring 1977), 131.
Welch believes that *On the Outside* and *On the*
Inside, performed successfully at the Peacock
Theatre in 1974, were "competently made, if somewhat
unsurprising," and he notes that they are set in
the 1950s and capture the "sex-laden atmosphere one
associates with the period."

II. REVIEWS

FAMINE

Billington, Michael. "Too Big a Famine." *The*
Times, 10 November 1969, p. 11.
Billington objects to the highly unflat-
tering picture of landowners offering mass
emigration as the only alternative to starva-
tion. On the other hand, he likes the compas-
sionate but impotent priests and the unsenti-
mentalized characterization of the poor. The
play needs and deserves a bigger production
than space at the Royal Court permits.

THE MORNING AFTER OPTIMISM

Roberts, Peter. "Optimism." *The Times*, 17 March
1974, p. 12.
This play compensates some for the awful-
ness of the previous week's festival offerings
(Dublin). Roberts writes, "By juxtaposing
romantic figures from the nursery world of
bedtime reading with two from the bedtime literature of the porn shop, Thomas Murphy had a
counterpoint working for him that gave the
dialogue a rippling, ironic detachment. This
is something dramatists who earnestly represent
life as a forest stand in some need of." He
praises especially the "inspired clowning of
Colin Blakely as the pimp."

Gussow, Mel. "'Morning After' Set in Irish Whimsey."
New York Times, 28 June 1974, p. 24.
This reviewer describes the American
premiere of the play in the Manhattan Theatre
Club. The story of "a pimp, his only prosti-
tute, a handsome prince, and an eager maiden"
is compared to *Green Mansions* and *A Midsummer*
Night's Dream. Gussow notes the *Irish Times*
called it the most original Irish play of the

past quarter of a century. He finds the play
"beguiling."

ON THE OUTSIDE/ON THE INSIDE

Barnes, Clive. New York Times, 9 March 1976, p. 27.
        While Barnes felt that A Whistle in the
Dark was a happy blend of O'Casey and Pinter,
he finds this double bill of Murphy one-acters
slight in content and dependent on atmosphere.
The topics of frustrated courtship and preg-
nancy out of wedlock are rather routinely de-
veloped.

Lewsen, Charles. "Conversation Before Acting." The
Times, 8 October 1974, p. 13.
        In general Lewsen pans the current festi-
val, but he considers On the Outside the best
of the plays offered although "the anecdote
is slight." He adds, "The dialogue, with its
wistful reference to the easy virtue of Protestant girls, and the detail of Murphy's production from the peeled paint advertisement for a
local grocer to the wiping of a greasy comb on
an oversized jacket, is [sic] lovingly precise."
He suggests, however, that the idea of the play
is hardly new; rather "it comes from Mr. Murphy's bottom drawer."

THE ORPHANS

Wardle, Irving. "Irish Residents and Exiles." The
Times, 12 October 1968, pp. 21, 23.
        The reviewer contrasts Murphy's new play
with A Whistle in the Dark, noting that the
current drama is "a piece which makes the circumstances of Irish birth seem like an incur-
able disease." Yet he adds that the playwright
"has done all he can to abandon national stereotypes. . . . Calculated flatness replaces
melodramatic climaxes; there is much talk about
happenings and LSD, and when anyone drops into
brogue it is only for purposes of contemptuous
mimicking." Wardle explains, however, that the
effect of this reversal is to make the play
more Irish than ever, evoking the old themes of
physical disgust and religious sentimentality.
Apart from Aideen O'Kelley's perfect production
it is on the whole "a fumbling affair."

THE SANCTUARY LAMP

Peter, John. "Delightful Debut." The Sunday Times,
12 October 1975, p. 37.
A favorable review in which Peter states
that "Clearly Mr. Murphy is contrasting divine
vigilance, if any, with the human misery that
goes undetected by it--and to which his play
is a substantial contribution." The reviewer
continues, "A statue of the Saviour looks on
in an attitude of anguished resignation with
which I have every sympathy."

SNAKES AND REPTILES

Billington, Michael. "When Exiles Come Home." The
Times, 15 February 1968, p. 6.
A review of the BBC 2 performance which
Billington considers "a moderately compelling
piece," although he notes that it is based on
"a return to the old theme of the inescapable
choice facing any young Irishman, between es-
cape to the freedom of England or acceptance
of the restrictions of the homeland." He states
that "even if the play took us through fairly
well-charted territory, it did at least convey
with some good raw tangy dialogue all the
prickly unease of a reunion with one's erst-
while chums." Along with the dialogue Billington praises the performances of Dudley Sutton
and Jim Norton.

A WHISTLE IN THE DARK

Barnes, Clive. New York Times, 17 February 1968,
p. 32.
The Long Wharf Theatre's American premiere
of Murphy's play impressed New Haven audiences
favorably. Barnes notes that it is "at first
glance a study of the face of violence. But
beneath the violence lie deeper issues of
family ties and blind loyalties, and the tragedy of a cowardly man ensnared by a situation
at least partly of his own making."

The Times, 12 September 1961, p. 14.
"Out of six brutes, one coward and one
bewildered girl Mr. Thomas Murphy makes a quite
terrifying play," writes this reviewer, who
adds, "While he (the playwright) is in control
of his story, he comes near to convincing us
that the whole world consists of stupid

fighting animals." Since the dramatist leads
us to expect that the father will be "unmasked"
at the end, the story loses its balance when he
is "left triumphant in his wickedness." Yet
the "lapse into commonplace melodrama" brings
the audience the relief of not necessarily be-
lieving in the dramatist's people. The cast is
excellent.

THE WHITE HOUSE

Lewsen, Charles. "An Exile's Return to the Past."
The Times, 22 March 1972, p. 9.
"At last the Dublin Theater Festival offers a contemporary Irish writer's encounter
with his identity as an Irishman," comments
this reviewer. Yet JJ, the hero, is "under-
characterized," and the boys and girls are
"really blank pages for JJ to write on." As a
result the characters lack "definition as people and as pieces in the design," thereby cre-
ating a situation where the audience "does not
easily focus on the characters at first sight."
The play needs cutting because it is too long,
especially in the second act before the an-
nouncement of Kennedy's death. For example,
"one kid's departure from JJ and his realiza-
tion that he hates his hero lacked power simply
because they had been delayed." Overall, the
direction, set, and lighting are excellent, and
"this is a resonant work by a writer of passion."

Edna O'Brien

Born December 15, 1932, Tuamgraney, Co. Clare.

Edna O'Brien deserves to be included in any book on contemporary Irish playwrights even though she is an expatriate and has written fewer plays than novels. In both drama and fiction she shares with Chekhov the technique of layering themes as if she were constructing a symphony while at the same time maintaining a naturalistic simplicity. Like the great Russian author, O'Brien is also a master of the short story form. More than fifteen years ago London recognized O'Brien's potential as a playwright when A Cheap Bunch of Nice Flowers was successfully staged. Ten years later A Pagan Place became her most impressive contribution to the theatre. It may well be the best analysis of a young Irish girl's sensibilities ever staged. Consistently O'Brien has contributed high quality television drama and film scripts. Much of her work has been censored in Ireland, due to her frank treatment of sexual matters; yet she is surprisingly traditional in her insistence on the lessons of history and the values of place in her characters' lives.

PRIMARY SOURCES

I. STAGE

A Cheap Bunch of Nice Flowers. Staged London, 1962.

_____. In Plays of the Year, vol. 26. Ed. J. C. Trewin. New York: Frederick Ungar, 1963.

"Last Rites of a Young Marriage." Vogue, 158 (July 1971), 92-93 (excerpt from Zee and Company).

A Pagan Place. Staged London, 1972.

_____. London: Faber and Faber, 1973.

The Wedding Dress. Mademoiselle, 58 (November 1963), 134-35.

Zee and Co. London: Weidenfeld and Nicolson, 1971.

II. TELEVISION (Exact dates of broadcast not available
                 from B.B.C. archives.)

Give My Love to the Pilchards, 1965.

The Keys of the Café, 1965.

Nothing's Ever Over, 1968.

Then and Now, 1973.

The Wedding Dress, 1963.

Which of These Two Ladies Is He Married to?, 1967.

III. FILM

The Girl with Green Eyes, 1964. Woodfall Films, A Tony
      Richardson production.

I Was Happy Here, 1966. J. Arthur Rank, A Roy Millichip
      production.

Three into Two Won't Go, 1968. Universal Pictures, A
      Julian Blaustein production.

X Y and Zee, 1972. Columbia Pictures, A Kastner-Ladd-
      Kanter production.

IV. FICTION

August Is a Wicked Month. London: Cape, 1964.

_____. New York: Simon and Schuster, 1965.

Casualties of Peace. London: Cape, 1965.

_____. New York: Simon and Schuster, 1967.

"Come into the Drawing-Room, Doris." New Yorker, 6 Octo-
      ber 1962, pp. 47-55.

_____. Winter's Tales, Vol. 9. Ed. A. D. Maclean.
      London: Macmillan, 1962. Pp. 143-76.

_____. The Love Object (under the title "Irish Revel").
      London: Cape, 1968.

"Cords." The Love Object. London: Cape, 1968; New
      York: Knopf, 1969. Pp. 131-48.

_____. The Sphere of Modern Irish Short Stories. Ed.
      David Marcus. London: Sphere, 1972.

The Country Girls. London: Hutchinson, 1960.

_____. New York: Knopf, 1962.

Girls in Their Married Bliss. London: Cape, 1964.

_____. Boston: Houghton Mifflin, 1968.

"Good Friday." Spectator, 25 April 1968, p. 522.

"How to Grow a Wisteria." The Love Object. London:
      Cape, 1968. Pp. 101-13.

"Let the Rest of the World Go By." Ladies Home Journal,
      82 (July 1965), 48-49.

_____. The Love Object (revised, under the title "How
      to Grow a Wisteria"). London: Cape, 1968.

The Lonely Girl. London: Cape, 1962.

_____. New York: Random House, 1962.

"The Love Object." New Yorker, 13 May 1957, pp. 42-52.

_____. The Love Object. London: Cape, 1968. Pp. 11-
      46.

The Love Object. London: Cape, 1968.

_____. New York: Knopf, 1969.

"Lovely to Look at, Delightful to Hold." New Yorker, 28
      March 1964), pp. 38-44.

_____. The Love Object (under the title "An Outing").
      London: Cape, 1968.

"The Lovers." New Yorker, 16 February 1963, pp. 28-34.

"My First Love." Ladies Home Journal, 82 (June 1965),
      60-61.

Night. London: Weidenfeld and Nicolson, 1972.

_____. New York: Knopf, 1973.

"An Outing." The Love Object. London: Cape, 1968. Pp. 47-69.

A Pagan Place. London: Weidenfeld and Nicolson, 1970.

_____. New York: Knopf, 1970.

"Paradise." The Love Object. London: Cape, 1968. Pp. 149-89.

"The Rug." New Yorker, 16 March 1963, pp. 55-57.

_____. The Love Object. London: Cape, 1968. Pp. 71-82.

A Scandalous Woman and Other Stories. London: Weidenfeld and Nicolson, 1974.

_____. New York: Harcourt Brace, 1974.

"Sister Imelda." Winter's Tales, vol. 9. Ed. A. D. Maclean. London: Macmillan, 1962.

_____. New York: St. Martin's Press, 1963. Pp. 170-92.

"Which of These Two Ladies Is He Married to?" New Yorker, 25 April 1964, pp. 49-54.

_____. The Love Object (under the title "Cords"). London: Cape, 1968.

"Women at the Seaside." Mademoiselle, 60 (March 1965), 168-69.

V. NONFICTION

"Dear Mr. Joyce." Audience, 1 (July-August 1971), 75-77.

VI. TRANSLATIONS

AUGUST IS A WICKED MONTH

   Agosto es un Mes Diabólico. Tr. by Mireia Bofill. Barcelona: Grijalbo, 1966. Spanish.

   Augusti är en Farlig Månao. Tr. by Gunilla Berglund. Stockholm: Forum, 1966. Swedish.

THE COUNTRY GIRLS

Country Girl. Tr. by Ôkubo Yasuo. Tokyo:
Shûeisha, 1966. Japanese.

Die Fünfzehnjährigen. Tr. by Jeannie Ebner. Ham-
burg: Rütten & Loening, 1961. German.

Irsk Blod. Tr. by Birgit Gjernes. Oslo: Gyldendal, 1960. Norwegian.

Irsk Uskyld. Tr. by Asta Hoff-Jørgensen. Copenhagen: Spektrum, 1961. Danish.

_____. Tr. by Asta Hoff-Jørgensen. Copenhagen:
Gyldendal (2. udg.), 1971. Danish.

La Jeune Islandaise. Tr. by Janine Michel. Paris:
Julliard, 1960. French.

Maalaistytöt. Tr. by Maini Palosuo. Helsinki:
Otava, 1961. Finnish.

Ragazze Di Campagna. Tr. by Vincenzo Mantovani.
Milano: Feltrinelli, 1961. Italian.

Tuå Flickor På Irland. Tr. by Karin Bong. Stockholm: Fritze, 1962. Swedish.

GIRLS IN THEIR MARRIED BLISS

Flickor I Äktenskapets Hamn. Tr. by Gunilla Berglund. Stockholm: Forum, 1965. Swedish.

Mädchen in Ehegluck. Tr. by Margaret Carroux.
Reinbeck: Rororo, 1972. German.

THE GIRL WITH GREEN EYES

Dziewczyna o zielonych oczach. Tr. by Maria Zborow-
ska. Warsaw: Wiedza, 1973. Polish.

Das Mädchen mit den Grünen Augen. Tr. by Margaret
Carroux. Wels: Welsermühl, 1972; Zurich:
Diogenes, 1972. German.

_____. Munich: DTU, 1974. German.

Het Meisje Met De Groene Ogen. Tr. by Catherine van
Eysden. 's-Grau.: Zuid. Holl. U. M., 1971.
Dutch.

99

Midori No Hitomi. Tr. by Kijima Jirô. Tokyo: Shûeisha, 1966. Japanese.

THE LONELY GIRL

Jeunes Filles Seules. Tr. by Daria Olivier. Paris: Presses de la Cité, 1962. French.

La Ragazza Sola. Tr. by Amalia D'Agostino Schanzer. Milano: Rizzoli, 1963. Italian.

Yalniz Kiz. Tr. by Seckin Selvi. Istanbul: Olus Yayinevi, 1972. Turkish.

THE LOVE OBJECT

Das Liebesobjekt. Tr. by Elisabeth Schnack. Zurich: Diogenes, 1972. German.

_____. Frankfurt: Fischer, 1977. German.

NIGHT

Nacht. Tr. by Frédérique van der Velde. Bussum: Agathon, 1974. Dutch.

A PAGAN PLACE

Et Hedensk Sted. Tr. by Margit Methling. Copen- hagen: Gyldendal, 1971. Danish.

Een Heidens Oord: Jaren van Onschuld. Tr. by Frédérique van der Velde. Bussum: Agathon, 1973. Dutch.

Les Païens D'Irlande. Tr. by Robert Giroux. Paris: Gallimard, 1973. French.

Pakannllinen Paikka. Tr. by Heidi Järuenpää. Hel- sinki: Otava. Finnish.

Aru Ai No Subete. Tr. by Aoki Hideo. Tokyo: Kado- kawa Shoten, 1972. Japanese.

ZEE AND CO.

X, Y, & Zee; oder, Deine Freundin ist bezaubernd. Tr. by Elisabeth Schnack. Zurich: Diogenes, 1972. German.

<u>Zee Och Vi</u>. Tr. by Solveig Nellinge. Stockholm: Trevi; Solna: Seelig, 1971. Swedish.

VII. INTERVIEWS

Bannon, Barbara. "Authors and Editors." <u>Publishers Weekly</u>, 25 May 1970, pp. 21-22.
  Bannon praises O'Brien's novel <u>A Pagan Place</u>, later to become a successful play. O'Brien speaks of the need for people "to get really back to a sense of a place in an almost atavistic sense," and tells how her reading of Joyce and encouragement by Paedar O'Donnell of <u>The Bell</u> contributed to her becoming a successful author.

Dunn, Nell, ed. "Edna." <u>Talking to Women</u>. London: MacGibbon and Kee, 1965. Pp. 69-107.
  O'Brien discusses her attitudes toward Ireland and her career as a writer. She defends her candid treatment of sex and feminist views. An informative, witty, relaxed discussion.

SECONDARY SOURCES

I. CRITICISM

Boyle, Patrick. "Edna O'Brien: A Touch of Rabelais." <u>Hibernia</u>, 17 April 1972, p. 17.
  Essentially a review of <u>A Pagan Place</u>, Boyle's article praises O'Brien's candor about sexual matters.

Cahill, Susan and Thomas Cahill. <u>A Literary Guide to Ireland</u>. New York: Scribner's, 1973. P. 118.
  The Cahills comment on Edna O'Brien's dreary landscapes, especially Tuamgraney.

Eckley, Grace. <u>Edna O'Brien</u>. Cranbury, N.J.: Associated University Presses, 1974.
  This book was written for the Irish Writer Series. It contains a chronology of O'Brien's life and a brief bibliography. It attempts to define O'Brien as a person. In many ways she seems bound by her Irish past and by guilt in sexual matters--although intellectually she has freed herself from provincial thinking. Eckley emphasizes O'Brien's novels rather than her plays.

Emerson, Sally. "Olivia Manning." Books and Bookmen,
17 (November 1971), 30-31.
    In this interview with Olivia Manning, Manning
    discusses the contemporary novel and certain of its
    major practitioners. Edna O'Brien is discussed as
    a woman writer "writing from the true feminine view-
    point."

Fallis, Richard. The Irish Renaissance. Syracuse:
    Syracuse University Press, 1977. Pp. 279-80.
    Fallis says that the Irish cliché "Edna O'Brien
    = sex" is unfair. She may be candid, but she cre-
    ated an important "record of the discontent of our
    fame and the emergence of a new consciousness among
    women."

Hogan, Robert. "Where Have All the Shamrocks Gone?" In
    Aspects of the Irish Theatre. Eds. Patrick Rafroidi,
    Raymonde Popot and William Parker. Lille: L'Univer-
    sité de Lille, 1972. P. 262.
    Hogan briefly alludes to O'Brien's censorship
    problems in Ireland.

Kenny, Herbert A. Literary Dublin: A History. Dublin:
    Gill and MacMillan, 1974. Pp. 270, 274, 303.
    Kenny is primarily concerned with O'Brien's
    novels but generally traces her problems with cen-
    sorship in Ireland to her feminist themes.

Kiely, Benedict. "The Whore on the Half-Doors." In
    Conor Cruise O'Brien Introduces Ireland. Ed. Owen
    Dudley Edwards. New York: McGraw-Hill, 1969.
    Pp. 148-61.
    This deals primarily with O'Brien's fiction but
    contains some insights into her treatment of women.

McMahon, Sean. "A Sex by Themselves: An Interim Report
    on the Novels of Edna O'Brien." Eire-Ireland, 2
    (Spring 1967), 79-87.
    Although he is critical of O'Brien's lapses
    into cynicism and suspicious of her feminism,
    McMahon generally praises her achievements as a
    novelist. All of her major works to date are sum-
    marized and her major themes are explored. The
    article is therefore very useful though O'Brien's
    plays as such are not discussed.

_____. "Books and Authors Today." Eire-Ireland, 1
    (Summer 1966), 85-88.
    O'Brien is mentioned as a prominent contempo-
    rary Irish literary talent. She is called "a kind
    of emotional suffragette."

_____. See Friel bibliography above.

Minnis, Alastair. "An Aspect of Edna O'Brien." Honest
Ulsterman, no. 21 (1970), pp. 27-31.

Popot, Raymonde. "Edna O'Brien's Paradise Lost."
Cahiers Irlandais, 4-5 (1976) 255-85.
   Popot describes the sense of alienation felt
by young Irish people, especially the women, towards
a nation which has failed to move into the modern
world. They cannot reconcile their heritage with
contemporary culture.

Pouillard, M. "Ames en peine: La solitude dans la
trilogie d'Edna O'Brien." Les Langues Modernes, 65
(July-August 1971), 365-73.
   The Country Girls, Girl with Green Eyes, and
Girls in Their Married Bliss show a progressive
pessimism and irony. O'Brien's heroines are
thwarted by life in Ireland but fear their loss of
individuality when they move away.

Rafroidi, Patrick. "Bovaryism and the Irish Novel,"
Irish University Review, 7 (Autumn 1977), 237-43.
   Although Rafroidi's primary concern here is
with the Irish novel, his comments on Edna O'Brien's
description of women are equally appropriate to the
author's dramatic portraits. O'Brien, he feels,
successfully satirizes the unnecessary martyrdom of
Irish women in a male-dominated society.

Senn, Fritz. "Reverberations." James Joyce Quarterly,
3 (Spring 1966), 222.
   Senn compares a passage in Dubliners with
The Country Girls to indicate Joyce's influence on
O'Brien.

Trevor, William. "Edna O'Brien." In Contemporary Novel-
ists. Ed. James Vinson. London: St. James Press,
1976. Pp. 1050-52.
   Although the focus of Trevor's brief survey
is on O'Brien's novels, he lists many other primary
sources, including drama, and he uses excerpts from
interviews with the author as well as a concise
analysis of her major themes and her place in modern
Irish literature.

II. REVIEWS

A CHEAP BUNCH OF NICE FLOWERS

The Times, 21 November 1962, p. 15.
It is hard to know what attitude the playwright wants us to adopt towards her characters, although she may be saying this is how
people act in such a situation, a confrontation
between mother and daughter. In any case, the
result is unsatisfactory, "for people do not
normally react to domestic stress with the
callous gaiety that makes mock of the dialogue." The tone increasingly "suggests black
forces," yet because Ria is onstage and not in
a novel, self-dramatization has to be shown, not
acted out in her mind, and thus "despite the
delicacy and truth in much of the writing, the
effect is forced and unnatural." The reviewer
notes of O'Brien's style that "the sympathetic
personal tone of the novels has vanished and
in its place is a combination of Chekhovian
obliqueness, and conventional theatricalism."
The actresses' performances are lauded.

THE GATHERING

Beauford, John. Christian Science Monitor, 21 March
1977, p. 22.
Beauford calls The Gathering a "bitter
family reunion" but finds it "searing family
drama, which mingles savage confrontations and
recriminations with moments of tenderness,
touching reminiscence and comic family fun and
games."

Gussow, Mel. New York Times, 11 March 1977, p.III:3.
The writing of the play is so filled with
bitterness and bad memories that it buries
the drama. It tells of several siblings' return home for their parents' fiftieth wedding
anniversary and hence evokes a situation similar to Storey's In Celebration, which is a
far superior treatment of the same theme.

Lewsen, Charles. "Dublin Theater Festival." The
Times, 11 October 1974, p. 17.
The reviewer writes, "one assumes that
Miss O'Brien is trying to use a contemporary
setting to give immediacy to grand passions."
Yet he feels that perhaps the direction is not
sensitive enough to allow full expression of

the playwright's intent. He states that this
is a play "where passion flares as inexplicably
from the final actions of its half-realized
characters as it does from the first."

A PAGAN PLACE

    Barnes, Clive. New York Times, 31 January 1974,
       p. 27.
         Barnes calls A Pagan Place "a remarkably
sensitive play, filled with a strange mixture
of anger and compassion." It reminds him of
The Prime of Miss Jean Brodie. Autobiographi-
cal elements abound and the feeling of Ireland,
"its pubs, its characters, its schools and its
mist," is everywhere. A high point is the scene
where the ailing mother says goodbye to her
fantasized relationship with the aging, alco-
holic doctor.

    Wardle, Irving. The Times, 3 November 1972, p. 11.
         Wardle comments that "in her freedom from
the literary revenge motive and from any im-
pulse to distort the past [Edna O'Brien] is a
most un-Irish artist; and her best qualities
are beautifully transmitted in this stage
version of her novel, A Pagan Place." He notes
that the play is "a delicate piece of impres-
sionism," reflecting the dramatist's "aim of
presenting ordinary life as an interesting
spectacle without falsifying it." Chekhovian
in its use of internal ironies and cross-refer-
ences, "the play emerges like a series of old
snapshots." He has high praise for the actress
who plays Creena and for the production as a
whole.

INDEX

This index includes authors (and co-authors) of secondary sources, including interviews, criticism, dissertations, and reviews. In addition, it includes translators of primary sources. The entry numbers refer to the page numbers.